Classic
and Retro

Straub's Manual of Mixed Drinks

A Facsimile of the 1913 Edition

Jacques Straub

Wine Steward of the Blackstone Hotel,
Chicago, Illinois. Formerly Manager of the Pendennis
Club, Louisville, Kentucky

Historic Cookbooks of the World
Kalevala Books
Chicago ❖ Phoenix

"No mixed drink is perfect unless ingredients used are perfect."
— Jacques Straub

Straub's Manual of Mixed Drinks:
A Facsimile of the 1913 Edition

Joanne Asala, Series Editor

Classic Cocktail Guides and Retro Bartender Books and *Historic Cookbooks of the World* are published by Kalevala Books, an imprint of Compass Rose Technologies, Inc. Titles published by Kalevala Books are available at special quantity discounts to use as premiums and sales promotions or for academic use. For more information, please e-mail us at editor@compassrose.com or write to:

Compass Rose Technologies, Inc.
PO Box 409095
Chicago, IL 60640

Editors' Note

Some ingredients found in vintage cocktail guides are unavailable or hard to come by today. Check out our resource guide at the back for vendors who specialize in hard-to-find ingredients and websites with information on how to recreate classic cocktails and cocktail ingredients.

ISBN: 978-1-880954-43-0

STRAUB'S MANUAL of MIXED DRINKS

Published by

R. FRANCIS WELSH PUBLISHING COMPANY

CHICAGO   ILLINOIS

A Complete Manual

of

Mixed Drinks

For All Occasions

THIS book contains over 675 clear and accurate directions for mixing all kinds of popular and fancy drinks, served in the best hotels, clubs, buffets, bars and homes. Added to this there is a splendid introduction on wines, their medicinal value, when and how to serve them, kinds and styles of glasses to use and other valuable information and facts of great importance to every user of wines and liquors.

By JACQUES STRAUB

Wine Steward of the Blackstone Hotel, Chicago.

Formerly manager of the Pendennis Club, Louisville, Ky.

Published by

R. FRANCIS WELSH PUBLISHING CO.

Chicago

THE AUTHOR
MR. JACQUES STRAUB

Mr. Jacques Straub

IT is, indeed, a rare art to skilfully combine and
mix certain drinks that will produce a beverage
the excellence of which is a real source of enjoyment to the most exacting palate.

There is perhaps no man in America to-day who
enjoys the enviable reputation of Jacques Straub
in this respect. As a celebrated connoisseur his
name is known and his recipes are used in the best
places of this country. His knowledge of wines and
liquors, how they are produced, how and when to
use them, is the result of a lifelong study and
years of practical experience in the wine and liquor
industry.

Mr. Straub is a native of Switzerland. In early
life he began a careful study of wine culture from
the vineyard to the table. He has practiced in all
its branches from the work in the field to the scientific study of soils, fermentation, maturing and
proper handling of wines. More than that, he has
gone deep into the therapeutical, hygienic properties and medicinal uses of alcoholic beverages.
While in Europe he visited the world-renowned wine
districts, made a study of the different methods of
production employed by the most celebrated wine
makers and distillers, and engaged practically in
the distillation of all the known liquors on the mar-
ket.

On leaving Europe, Mr. Straub went to Louisville,
Ky., where he was soon given charge of the wine
department of the Pendennis Club. As wine steward and manager for twenty-one years he made the
wine cellars of that place famous for their wonderful selection of vintages.

It was only natural for Straub, being located in the

Blue Grass Region, to at once begin the study of Rye and Bourbon distillation, which, with his usual analytic thoroughness he soon mastered. Scientific distillation of liquors as pursued to-day by the big institutions is an art to be acquired only by long years of experimenting, endless research in perfecting methods and processes, besides an accurate knowledge of maturing and developing the product to the highest degree of purity. Mr. Straub is firm in these points, having early in his career adopted a policy of never endorsing any product which he knows from his own analysis, does not live up to the most approved ideas of manufacture. He believes a drink must not only be a pleasure to the palate but so made that its effect on the stomach will be health-giving and invigorating.

When the Blackstone Hotel of Chicago was erected, the owners had in mind one determined idea, that of making the wonderful structure the embodiment of the best in modern hotel comfort. They planned to build up an institution that would arouse the interest of the whole world for its luxurious apartments, well appointed dining rooms, grill room, and unexcelled wine cellar and store rooms. To get the best of these things they sought the best talent—men of known reputation and fame in their particular lines—to install and take charge of the departments. Mr. Straub, whose reputation as manager of the Pendennis Club was well known in the Hotel World, was asked to establish their wine cellar and act as wine steward. With his long experience in this work, keen understanding of the high class of patronage the Blackstone would cater to, and his knowledge of wines and liquors, he soon succeeded in putting in wine cellars that are not excelled by any hotel in the world for their wonderful selection of vintages and perfect management.

Mr. Straub never stops at the price in buying his wines or liquors. He appreciates perhaps more than any other man the value of quality in a celebrated institution like the Blackstone.

As an authority on alcoholic beverages, how to care for them, when and how to use them, his reputation is unsurpassed.

Mr. Straub is a man of interesting personality. He gets down to the closest analysis of his subject and completes it with a thoroughness that can't help but be successful. In compiling these hundreds of mixed drinks he has used that same thoroughness, talent and understanding characteristic of his usual work.

THE PUBLISHERS.

COBBLERS

CLARET COBBLER.

Fill Goblet with fine ice.
½ Jigger Syrup.
½ Jigger Claret.
Stir, decorate with fruit.

PORT WINE COBBLER.

Fill Goblet with fine ice.
⅓ Jigger Syrup.
1½ Jiggers Port Wine.
Stir, decorate with fruit.

RHINE WINE COBBLER.

Fill Goblet with fine ice.
1½ Jiggers Rhine Wine.
½ Jigger Syrup.
2 Drops Lemon Juice.
Stir, decorate with fruit.

SHERRY COBBLER.

Fill Goblet with fine ice.
1 Jigger Sherry.
½ Jigger Syrup.
1 Lemon Peel.
Stir, decorate with fruit.

WHISKEY COBBLER.

Fill Goblet with fine ice.
1 Jigger Green River Whiskey.
¼ Jigger Curacao.
1 Slice of Lemon.
Decorate with fruit.

COCKTAILS

Serve in Cocktail glass unless otherwise specified

ABSINTHE COCKTAIL
¾ Jigger Green Absinthe.
1 Dash Orange and Angostura Bitters.
1 Dash Anisette.
Shake well.
Serve.

ADONIS COCKTAIL
2 Dashes Orange Bitters.
⅓ Jigger Sherry.
⅔ Jigger Italian Vermouth.
Stir.

ALASKA COCKTAIL
1 Dash Orange Bitters.
⅓ Jigger Yellow Chartreuse.
⅔ Jigger Tom Gin.
Shake.

ALEXANDER COCKTAIL
¾ Jigger Rye Whiskey.
¼ Jigger Benedictine.
Twist Orange Peel on top.
Stir.

ANDERSON COCKTAIL
¼ Jigger Italian Vermouth.
¾ Jigger Dry Gin.
Stir well.
Orange Peel.

APPLEJACK COCKTAIL
1 Dash Orange Bitters.
1 Jigger Apple Brandy.
Squeeze piece Lemon Peel in mixing glass.
Frappé.
Olive.

ARDSLEY COCKTAIL
½ Jigger Calisaya.
½ Jigger Sloe Gin.
Shake.

ARMOUR COCKTAIL
1 Dash Orange Bitters.
½ Jigger Italian Vermouth.
½ Jigger Sherry.
Stir.

ASTORIA COCKTAIL
1 Dash Orange Bitters.
⅔ Jigger Tom Gin.
⅓ Jigger French Vermouth.
Stir.

AUTO COCKTAIL
⅓ Jigger French Vermouth.
⅓ Jigger Tom Gin.
⅓ Jigger Scotch Whiskey.
Shake.

AVIATION COCKTAIL
¾ Jigger Apple Jack.
½ Jigger Lime Juice.
1 Dash Absinthe.
1 Barspoonful of Grenadine Syrup.
Shake.

BALLANTINE COCKTAIL
1 Dash Absinthe.
⅓ Jigger French Vermouth.
⅔ Jigger Dry Gin.
Shake.

BAMBOO COCKTAIL
⅓ Jigger Italian Vermouth.
⅔ Jigger Dry Sherry.
1 Dash Orange Bitters.

BARACCAS COCKTAIL
¾ Jigger Italian Vermouth.
¼ Jigger Fernet-Branca.

BARRY COCKTAIL

> 2 Dashes Angostura Bitters.
> 4 Dashes Creme de Menthe.
> ½ Jigger Italian Vermouth.
> ½ Jigger Dry Gin.

BEADLESTONE COCKTAIL

> ½ Jigger McCallum's Perfection Scotch Whiskey.
> ½ Jigger French Vermouth.
> Shake.

BEALS COCKTAIL

> ½ Jigger Scotch Whiskey.
> ¼ Jigger French Vermouth.
> ¼ Jigger Italian Vermouth.
> Shake.
> Serve in whiskey glass.

BEAUTY COCKTAIL

> ½ Jigger High and Dry Gin.
> ¼ Jigger French Vermouth.
> ¼ Jigger Italian Vermouth.
> 1 White of an Egg.
> 1 Dash of Absinthe.
> 1 Barspoonful Syrup.
> Shake.

BEAUTY SPOT COCKTAIL

> ⅛ Jigger Orange Juice.
> ¼ Jigger Italian Vermouth.
> ¼ Jigger French Vermouth.
> ½ Jigger Gin.
> Dash of Grenadine bottom of glass.

BIJOU COCKTAIL

> ⅓ Jigger Green Chartreuse.
> ⅓ Jigger Dry Gin.
> ⅓ Jigger Italian Vermouth.
> Shake.

BIRD COCKTAIL
⅔ Jigger Brown Curacao.
⅓ Jigger Brandy.
Shake well.

BISHOP POTTER COCKTAIL
2 Dashes Orange Bitters.
2 Dashes Calisaya.
¼ Jigger French Vermouth.
¼ Jigger Italian Vermouth.
½ Jigger Dry Gin.
Stir well.

BISHOP COCKTAIL
1 Jigger Jamaica Rum.
1 Barspoon Syrup.
1 Barspoon Claret.
1 Dash Lemon Juice.
Shake.

BLACK HAWK COCKTAIL
½ Jigger Rye Whiskey.
½ Jigger Sloe Gin.
Stir.
1 Cherry.

BLACKSTONE COCKTAIL
¼ Jigger Italian Vermouth.
¼ Jigger French Vermouth.
½ Jigger Dry Gin.
1 Piece Orange Peel.
Shake.

BLACKSTONE NO. 1
¼ Jigger Italian Vermouth.
¾ Jigger Booth's Old Tom Gin.
Shake.
Squeeze Lemon Peel on top.

BLACKTONE NO. 2
(Special Blackstone.)
⅓ Jigger French Vermouth.
⅔ Jigger Dry Gin.
Serve with Orange Peel on top.

BLACKSTONE NO. 3 SPECIAL
1 Dash Absinthe.
⅓ Jigger French Vermouth.
⅔ Jigger Dry Gin.
Serve with Lemon Peel on top.

BLACKTHORNE COCKTAIL
1 Dash Orange Bitters.
⅓ Jigger Italian Vermouth.
⅔ Jigger Sloe Gin.
Lemon Peel.

BOBBIE BURNS COCKTAIL
(For Two.)
1 Barspoonful Orange Juice.
1 Barspoonful Maraschino.
Crush 1 Lump of Sugar.
½ Jigger Scotch.
½ Jigger Italian Vermouth.
Shake.

BOLES COCKTAIL
¼ Jigger Italian Vermouth.
¼ Jigger French Vermouth.
½ Jigger Dry Gin.
Ice.
Stir.
1 Orange Peel.
Serve in old fashion glass.

BOOBY COCKTAIL
1 Jigger Gin.
⅛ Jigger Grenadine Syrup.
½ Jigger Lime Juice.
Shake well in Fine Ice.

BRANDY COCKTAIL
2 Dashes Orange Bitters.
1 Jigger good Brandy.
2 Dashes Plain Syrup.
Stir.

BRANT COCKTAIL
1 Dash Angostura.
¼ Jigger White Mint.
¾ Jigger Brandy.
Lemon Peel on top.
Shake.

BRIDAL COCKTAIL
1 Dash Orange Bitters.
⅓ Jigger Italian Vermouth.
⅔ Jigger Dry Gin.
1 Dash Maraschino (Holland.)
Stir well.
Orange Peel on top.

BRIGHTON COCKTAIL
1 Dash Orange Bitters.
½ Jigger Italian Vermouth.
¼ Jigger Dry Gin.
¼ Jigger Tom Gin.
1 Lemon Peel.
Stir well.

BROOKLYN COCKTAIL
1 Dash Amer Picon.
1 Dash Maraschino.
½ Jigger French Vermouth.
½ Jigger good Rye Whiskey.
Stir.

BRONX COCKTAIL
½ Jigger Dry Gin.
¼ Jigger Italian Vermouth.
¼ Jigger French Vermouth.
1 Piece Orange.
Shake well.

BRONX DRY
½ Jigger High and Dry Gin.
½ Jigger Noilly Prat & Co. Vermouth.
1 Barspoonful Orange Juice.
Shake.

BRONX TERRACE
Juice of ½ Lime.
½ Jigger Dry Gin.
½ Jigger French Vermouth.
Shake.

BROWN COCKTAIL
1 Dash Orange Bitters.
⅔ Jigger Rye Whiskey.
⅓ Jigger Dry Gin.
Shake.

BRUT COCKTAIL (French Style.)
4 Dashes Angostura Bitters.
⅓ Jigger Amer Picon.
⅔ Jigger French Vermouth.
Stir well.

BRUT COCKTAIL
½ Jigger French Vermouth.
½ Jigger Calisaya.
1 Dash Absinthe.
Shake.

BUSCH COCKTAIL
½ Jigger Italian Vermouth.
½ Jigger High and Dry Gin.
1 Barspoonful Apple Brandy.
Shake.

BYRRH COCKTAIL
¼ Jigger Vermouth.
¼ Jigger Rye Whiskey.
½ Jigger Byrrh Wine.

CABINET COCKTAIL
½ Jigger French Vermouth.
½ Jigger Dry Gin.
Orange Peel.
Shake.

CAFE DE PAREE COCKTAIL

1 Jigger High and Dry Gin.
1 White of Egg.
1 Barspoon Cream.
1 Barspon Anisette.
Frappe.
Serve in Claret glass.

CAFE AU KIRSCH

1 Pony Kirschwasser.
1 Pony Martell Brandy.
1 White of Egg.
1 Pony Cold Black Coffee.
Frappe.
Serve in Claret glass.

CALISAYA COCKTAIL

1 Jigger Calisaya.
1 Dash Angostura Bitters.
Stir.

CALUMET CLUB COCKTAIL

3 Dashes of Acid Phosphate.
1 Dash Angostura Bitters.
½ Jigger Green River Whiskey.
½ Jigger Italian Vermouth.
Stir.

CAMEO KIRBY COCKTAIL

½ Jigger Dry Gin.
½ Jigger French Vermouth.
2 Barspoons Raspberry Syrup.
5 Drops Lime Juice.
Shake.

CAT COCKTAIL

½ Jigger French Vermouth.
½ Jigger Dry Gin.
Stir.
Olive.

C. A. W. COCKTAIL

⅓ Jigger Italian Vermouth.
⅓ Jigger French Vermouth.
⅓ Jigger Brandy.
1 Piece of Orange Peel on top.
Shake.

CHAMPAGNE COCKTAIL
1 Lump of Sugar.
2 Dashes Angostura Bitters.
1 Dash Peychaud Bitters.
1 Piece of Orange Peel twisted on top.
1 Pint Champagne which customer selects.

CHANTECLER COCKTAIL
Bronx with 4 Dashes of Grenadine Syrup.
Shake.

CHAUNCEY COCKTAIL
¼ Jigger Brandy.
¼ Jigger Dry Gin.
¼ Jigger Italian Vermouth.
¼ Jigger Green River Whiskey.
Shake.

CHOCOLATE COCKTAIL
⅓ Jigger Maraschino.
⅓ Jigger Yellow Chartreuse.
⅓ Jigger Blackberry Brandy.
1 Yolk of Egg.
Shake.

CHRISP COCKTAIL
1 Dash Orange Bitters.
½ Jigger Dry Gin.
½ Jigger Italian Vermouth.
1 Slice of Orange.
Shake.

CIDER COCKTAIL
Lemon Rind.
2 Dashes Angostura Bitters.
1 Lump of Ice.
1 Pint Cider.

CINCINNATI COCKTAIL
½ Glass Beer.
Fill up with Soda or Ginger Ale.
Serve.

CLARE COCKTAIL

½ Jigger Sloe Gin.
½ Jigger Italian Vermouth.
Dash of Brandy on top.
Stir well.

CLOVE COCKTAIL

½ Jigger Italian Vermouth.
½ Jigger Sloe Gin.
1 Barspoon Brandy.
Shake.

CLOVER LEAF COCKTAIL

Juice of ½ a Lemon.
White of One Egg.
1 Jigger Dry Gin.
1 Barspoon Raspberry Syrup.
Shake well.
1 Sprig of Mint on top.

CLIFTON COCKTAIL

1 Dash Angostura Bitters.
1 Dash Brown Curacao.
½ Jigger Rye Whiskey.
½ Jigger French Vermouth.
Stir.

C. O. D. COCKTAIL

2 Dashes Grenadine.
1 Jigger Gin.
1 Slice Grape Fruit.
Shake.

COFFEE COCKTAIL

½ Teaspoonful of Sugar.
1 Egg.
½ Jigger Port Wine.
½ Jigger Brandy.
Shake well.
Serve in Claret glass.

COLUMBUS COCKTAIL

¾ Jigger French Vermouth.
¼ Jigger Angostura Bitters.
Shake well.

COLONIAL OR MILLER COCKTAIL
(For Two Persons.)

½ Jigger Maraschino.
1 Jigger Tom Gin.
1 Jigger Grape Fruit Juice.
Shake well.
Serve in Claret glass.

CONSOLIDATED COCKTAIL

¾ Jigger Dry Gin.
¼ Jigger M. & R. Italian Vermouth.

CONEY COCKTAIL

½ Jigger French Vermouth.
⅔ Jigger Dry Gin.
Shake well.

CONGRESS COCKTAIL

1 Pony Brandy.
1 Pony Creme de Rose.
3 Dashes Orange Flower Water.
1 White of Egg.
Shake.
Serve in Claret glass.

CORNELL COCKTAIL

⅓ Jigger French Vermouth.
½ Jigger Dry Gin.
Shake.

CORONATION COCKTAIL

⅓ Jigger French Vermouth.
⅓ Jigger Dry Gin.
⅓ Jigger Dubonnet.
Serve.

CREOLE COCKTAIL

⅓ Jigger Absinthe.
¾ Jigger Italian Vermouth.
Shake well.

CRISTIE COCKTAIL
2 Dashes Orange Bitters.
½ Jigger Dry Gin.
½ Jigger French Vermouth.
1 Piece of Lemon Peel.
Stir.

CUBAN COCKTAIL
½ Jigger Lime Juice.
⅓ Jigger Gin.
⅓ Jigger Brandy.
½ Jigger Apricot Brandy.
Shake.

CUSHMAN COCKTAIL
¼ Jigger French Vermouth.
¾ Jigger High and Dry Gin.
Shake.

DAIGUIRI COCKTAIL
⅔ Jigger Lime Juice.
⅓ Jigger Rum.
1 Barspon Powdered Sugar.
Shake well in fine ice and strain into
Cocktail glass.

DELMONICO COCKTAIL
½ Jigger French Vermouth.
½ Jigger Dry Gin.
1 Orange Peel.
Shake.

DIMENTION COCKTAIL
¼ Jigger Creme de Menthe White.
¼ Jigger Brandy.
½ Jigger Creme de Cacao.
Shake.

DORR COCKTAIL
⅔ Jigger Dry Gin.
⅓ Jigger Italian Vermouth.
2 Dashes French Vermouth.
Orange Peel.
Shake.

DOWN COCKTAIL

1 Dash Orange Bitters.
⅓ Jigger Italian Vermouth.
⅔ Jigger High and Dry Gin.
Stir.
Olive.

DREAM COCKTAIL

Juice of one-half a Lemon.
1 Barspoonful of Sugar.
¾ Jigger Dry Gin.
1 White of Egg.
1 Dash of Liqueur.
Shake.
Serve in Claret glass.

DRY MARTINI COCKTAIL

½ Jigger French Vermouth.
½ Jigger Booth's High and Dry Gin.
Stir.

DUBONNET COCKTAIL

½ Jigger Dry Gin.
½ Jigger Dubonnet.
1 Dash Orange Bitters.
Shake.

DUCHESS COCKTAIL

⅓ Jigger Italian Vemouth.
¼ Jigger French Vermouth.
⅓ Jigger Absinthe.
Shake well.

DUKE COCKTAIL

⅓ Jigger French Vermouth.
⅔ Jigger High and Dry Gin.
Stir.

DUPLEX OR ALBERN COCKTAIL

2 Dashes Orange Bitters.
½ Jigger Italian Vermouth.
½ Jigger French Vermouth.
Shake.

DUTCH CHARLIE'S COCKTAIL
2 Dashes Augostura Bitters.
⅓ Jigger Rye Whiskey.
⅓ Jigger Dubonnet.
⅓ Jigger Italian Vermouth.
Stir well.

EMERALD COCKTAIL
1 Dash Orange Bitters.
½ Jigger Italian Vermouth.
½ Jigger Irish Whiskey.
Stir.

EMERSON COCKTAIL
½ Lime Juice.
3 Dashes Maraschino.
⅓ Jigger Italian Vermouth.
½ Jigger Old Tom Gin.
Shake.

EVANS COCKTAIL
1 Dash Apricot Brandy.
1 Dash Curacao.
1 Jigger Rye Whiskey.
Stir.

EWING COCKTAIL
3 Dashes Angostura Bitters.
1 Jigger Rye Whiskey.
Stir.

EXPRESS COCKTAIL
1 Dash Orange Bitters.
½ Jigger Italian Vermouth.
½ Jigger McCallum's Perfection Scotch
Whiskey.
Shake.

FAIRBANK'S COCKTAIL
10 Dashes Apricot Brandy.
1 Jigger Rye Whiskey.
1 Dash Angostura Bitters.
Serve in old fashion glass.

FANCY BRANDY, GIN AND WHISKEY COCKTAILS

1 Dash of Syrup.
1 Dash Curacao.
1 Dash Angostura Bitters.
1 Jigger Brandy, Gin or Whiskey.
Shake.
Twist a piece of Lemon Peel.

FARMER'S COCKTAIL

3 Dashes Angostura Bitters.
½ Jigger Dry Gin.
¼ Jigger French Vermouth.
¼ Jigger Italian Vermouth.
Shake well.

FLUSHING COCKTAIL

⅓ Jigger Italian Vermouth.
⅔ Jigger Brandy.
1 Dash Syrup.
1 Dash Angostura Bitters.
1 Lemon Peel.
Stir.
Strain into old fashion glass and serve.

FOUR DOLLAR COCKTAIL

½ Jigger Dry Gin.
¼ Jigger French Vermouth.
¼ Jigger Italian Vermouth.

FOURTH REGIMENT COCKTAIL

1 Dash Orange Bitters.
1 Dash Angostura Bitters.
1 Dash Celery Bitters.
½ Jigger Whiskey.
½ Jigger Italian Vermouth.
Piece of Lemon Peel.
Shake.

FOURTH DEGREE OR FEATHER COCKTAIL

⅓ Jigger Noilly Prat Vermouth.
⅓ Jigger Martini & Rossi Vermouth.
⅓ Jigger White Absinthe.
Shake well.

FRANK HILL COCKTAIL

½ Jigger Cherry Brandy.
½ Jigger Martell Brandy.
Twist Lemon Peel.
Shake well.

FOX SHOT COCKTAIL

⅕ Jigger Angostura Bitters.
⅕ Jigger Brandy.
⅕ Jigger Italian Vermouth.
⅖ Jigger Dry Gin.
Stir well.

FRENCH CANADIAN COCKTAIL

1 Dash of Absinthe.
½ Jigger French Vermouth.
½ Jigger Canadian Whiskey.
Stir well.

FUTURITY COCKTAIL

2 Dashes Angostura Bitters.
½ Jigger Italian Vermouth.
½ Jigger Sloe Gin.
Stir.

GIBSON COCKTAIL

½ Jigger Noilly, Prat Vermouth.
½ Jigger High and Dry Gin.
Stir, strain and serve.

GIN COCKTAIL

1 Jigger Gin, whichever customers ask for.
1 or 2 Dashes Orange Bitters.
Stir well and serve.

GOLF COCKTAIL
⅓ Jigger French Vermouth.
⅔ Jigger Dry Gin.
2 Dashes Angostura Bitters.
Stir well and strain into cocktail glass.

GOOD FELLOW COCKTAIL
½ Jigger Italian Vermouth.
½ Jigger Green River Bourbon.
1 Dash Angostura Bitters.
1 Dash Calisaya.
Stir well, strain and serve.

GOOD TIMES COCKTAIL
⅓ Jigger French Vermouth.
⅔ Jigger Tom Gin.
1 Piece of Lemon Peel.
Shake and strain into cocktail glass.

GRAHAM COCKTAIL
¼ Jigger French Vermouth.
¾ Jigger Martini & Rossi Vermouth.
Stir well and strain.
Serve.

GRIT COCKTAIL
½ Jigger Italian Vermouth.
½ Jigger Irish Whiskey.
Shake, strain into cocktail glass.
Serve.

GUGGENHEIM COCKTAIL
1 Jigger French Vermouth.
2 Dashes Fernet Branca Bitters.
1 Dash Orange Bitters.
Shake, strain into Cocktail glass.
Serve.

HALL COCKTAIL
⅓ Jigger Italian Vermouth.
⅓ Jigger French Vermouth.
⅓ Jigger Booth's High and Dry Gin.
Stir.
Olive.

HART COCKTAIL
⅓ Jigger Gin.
⅓ Jigger Dubonnet.
⅓ Jigger Italian Vermouth.
Serve.

HARVARD COCKTAIL
2 Dashes Orange Bitters.
⅔ Jigger Sherry or Brandy.
⅓ Jigger Italian Vermouth.
1 Piece of Lemon Peel on top.
Stir well and serve.

HARVESTER COCKTAIL
½ Jigger Orange Juice.
½ Jigger Gin.
Shake.

HEARST COCKTAIL
1 Dash Angostura Bitters.
2 Dashes Orange Bitters.
½ Jigger High and Dry Gin.
½ Jigger Italian Vermouth.
Serve.

HIGHSTEPPER COCKTAIL
⅓ Jigger French Vermouth.
⅔ Jigger Dry Gin.
2 Dashes Angostura Bitters.
Shake.

HIGHLAND COCKTAIL
½ Jigger Italian Vermouth.
½ Jigger McCallum's Perfection Scotch
Whiskey.
Shake.

HILLARD COCKTAIL
2 Dashes Angostura Bitters.
⅓ Jigger Italian Vermouth.
⅔ Jigger Dry Gin.

HOLSTEIN COCKTAIL

1 Dash Amer Picon
½ Jigger Martell Cognac.
½ Jigger Blackberry Brandy.
Serve.

HOMESTEAD COCKTAIL

¼ Jigger Italian Vermouth.
⅔ Jigger Dry Gin.
Slice Orange.
Shake.

HONOLULU COCKTAIL

3 Dashes Angostura Bitters.
1 Jigger Green River Whiskey.
Add Seltzer.
Stir well and serve.

HOWARD COCKTAIL

Gin Cocktail.
1 Dash Angostura on top.

HUDSON COCKTAIL

¼ Jigger Italian Vermouth.
¾ Jigger Gin.
Slice Orange.
Serve.

HUNTER COCKTAIL

⅔ Jigger Rye Whiskey.
¼ Jigger Cherry Brandy.
Stir.

IMPROVED MARTINI COCKTAIL

Same as Martini Cocktail only add two
dashes Maraschino.
Shake.

INFURIATOR COCKTAIL
⅔ Jigger Brandy.
⅓ Jigger Anisette.
Shake well.
Strain into Cocktail glass.

IRIS COCKTAIL
⅓ Jigger Lemon Juice.
⅔ Jigger Gin.
1 Barspoonful Sugar.
Shake.
3 Sprigs of Mint.

IRVING COCKTAIL
½ Jigger Dry Gin.
¼ Jigger Calisaya.
¼ Jigger French Vermouth.
1 Slice Orange.
Shake.

ISABELLE COCKTAIL
1 Small lump of ice in cocktail glass.
½ Jigger Grenadine Syrup.
½ Jigger Creme de Cassis.

ITALIAN COCKTAIL
½ Jigger Italian Vermouth.
¼ Jigger Grenadine Syrup.
¼ Jigger Fernet Branca.

JACK ROSE COCKTAIL
1 Jigger Apple Jack.
½ Lime.
¼ Jigger Grenadine Syrup.
Shake well.

JACK ZELLER COCKTAIL
½ Jigger Booth's Old Tom Gin.
½ Jigger Dubonnet.
Stir.

JAPANESE COCKTAIL

2 Dashes Curacao.
½ Jigger Italian Vermouth.
⅓ Jigger Rye Whiskey.
⅙ Jigger Grenadine Syrup.
Shake.

JENKS COCKTAIL

Dry Martini with one Dash Benedictine.

JERSEY COCKTAIL

2 Dashes Syrup.
1 Jigger Apple Brandy.
2 Dashes Angostura Bitters.

JERSEY LILY COCKTAIL

Martini with Mint Sprigs.

JIM LEE COCKTAIL

2 Dashes Peychaud Bitters.
2 Dashes Angostura Bitters.
½ Jigger Dry Gin.
¼ Jigger French Vermouth.
¼ Jigger Italian Vermouth.
Shake.

JOCKEY CLUB COCKTAIL

Same as Gin Cocktail.

JOHN COCKTAIL

⅓ Jigger Italian Vermouth.
⅓ Jigger French Vermouth.
⅓ Jigger Gin.
White of one Egg.
Shake well.

JUDGE COCKTAIL

⅞ Jigger Rye Whiskey.
⅛ Jigger Apricot Brandy.
Shake.

JUNKINS COCKTAIL

¼ Jigger Italian Vermouth.
¾ Jigger Dry Gin or Rye Whiskey.
In small Whiskey Glass.
Small piece of Ice.
Lemon Peel.
Small Spoon.

KENTUCKY COLONEL COCKTAIL

¼ Jigger Benedictine.
¾ Jigger Green River Whiskey.
1 Piece of Lemon Peel.
Stir well and serve in an old style glass.

LEONORA COCKTAIL

¼ Jigger Orange Juice.
¼ Jigger Raspberry Syrup.
½ Jigger Dry Gin.
Serve.

LEWIS COCKTAIL

½ Jigger French Vermouth.
½ Jigger Dry Gin.
Shake.

LIBERAL COCKTAIL

⅓ Jigger Italian Vermouth.
⅔ Jigger Rye Whiskey.
1 Dash Amer Picon.
Stir.

LOEWI COCKTAIL

¼ Jigger French Vermouth.
¼ Jigger Orange Gin, Booth's.
½ Jigger Dry Gin.
Frappe.

LOFTUS COCKTAIL

Same as Duchess Cocktail.

LONE TREE COCKTAIL

⅓ Jigger Italian Vermouth.
⅔ Jigger Booth's Tom Gin.
Shake well.

LOVE COCKTAIL
Martini with White of Egg.
Shake.

LUSITANIA COCKTAIL
1 Dash Orange Bitters.
1 Dash Absinthe.
⅔ Jigger French Vermouth.
¼ Jigger Good Brandy.
Shake.

MALLORY COCKTAIL
⅓ Jigger Brandy.
⅓ Jigger Apricot Brandy.
⅓ Jigger White Creme de Menthe.
1 Dash Absinthe.
Shake.

MANHATTAN COCKTAIL
1 Dash Angostura Bitters.
⅓ Jigger Martini & Rossi Vermouth.
⅔ Jigger Green River Whiskey.
Stir.

MANHATTAN, JR., COCKTAIL
Manhattan with Orange Peel.
Shake well.

MARCONI COCKTAIL
⅓ Jigger Italian Vermouth
⅔ Jigger Apple Brandy.
Shake.

MARGUERITE COCKTAIL
½ Jigger French Vermouth.
2 Dashes Orange Bitters.
½ Jigger Dry Gin.
Stir.

MARQUERAY COCKTAIL
½ Lime Juice.
1 Dash Absinthe.
2 Dashes Grenadine Syrup.
1 White of Egg.
1 Jigger Dry Gin.
Shake.

MARTINI COCKTAIL
⅓ Jigger Martini & Rossi Italian Vermouth.
⅔ Jigger Gin.
1 Dash Orange Bitters.
Stir well and serve.

MAUSER COCKTAIL
½ Jigger Italian Vermouth.
½ Jigger Dry Gin.
1 Barspoonful Apple Brandy.
Shake.

McCUTCHEON COCKTAIL
1 Dash Orange Bitters.
1 Dash Angostura Bitters.
½ Jigger Dry Gin.
¼ Jigger French Vermouth.
¼ Jigger Italian Vermouth.
1 Dash Anisette on top.
Stir well and serve.

McHENRY COCKTAIL
Martini Cocktail with one Barspoonfull of
Hungarian Apricot Brandy.
Shake well and serve.

McLANE COCKTAIL
Same as Perfect Cocktail.

MERRY WIDOW COCKTAIL
4 Dashes Maraschino.
⅓ Jigger French Vermouth.
⅔ Jigger Italian Vermouth   or   Byrrh
Wine.
Shake well.

METROPOLITAN COCKTAIL
½ Jigger French Vermouth.
½ Jigger Brandy.
2 Dashes Angostura Bitters.
Stir.

METROPOLITAN COCKTAIL
(Southern Style.)
⅓ Jigger Italian Vermouth.
⅔ Jigger Brandy.
1 Dash Orange Bitters.
Serve.

MILLIONAIRE COCKTAIL
1 Dash Orange Bitters.
6 Dashes Curacao.
¾ Jigger Rye Whiskey.
2 Dashes Grenadine Syrup.
1 White of Egg.
Stir well.
Serve in Claret Glass.

MILLER COCKTAIL
Same as Colonial Cocktail.

MILO COCKTAIL
2 Dashes Pepsin Bitters.
⅓ Jigger Italian Vermouth.
⅔ Jigger Dry Gin.
Stir.

MONTANA COCKTAIL
¼ Jigger French Vermouth.
½ Jigger Brandy.
2 Dashes Port Wine.
2 Dashes Angostura Bitters.
2 Dashes Anisette.
Shake well.

MORNING COCKTAIL
1 Dash Absinthe.
1 Dash Angostura Bitters.
½ Jigger Brandy.
½ Jigger Italian Vermouth.
Frappe.

NANA COCKTAIL
1 White of Egg.
1 Barspoon Sugar.
1 Jigger Brandy.
Shake.

NARRAGANSETT COCKTAIL

⅔ Jigger Rye Whiskey.
⅓ Jigger Italian Vermouth.
1 Dash Absinthe.
Olive.
Stir well.

NETHERLAND COCKTAIL

⅓ Jigger Curacao.
⅔ Jigger Good Brandy.
1 Dash Orange Bitters.
Stir well.

NEWMAN COCKTAIL

3 Dashes Amer Picon
½ Jigger Dry Gin.
½ Jigger French Vermouth.
Shake.

NICHOLAS COCKTAIL

½ Jigger Sloe Gin.
½ Jigger Booth's Old Tom Gin.
Shake well.

NORTH POLE COCKTAIL

⅓ Jigger Maraschino.
⅓ Jigger Dry Gin.
Juice of one-half a Lemon.
1 White of Egg.
Shake well and strain into Claret glass
with whipped cream on top.

NUTTING COCKTAIL

1 Dash Angostura Bitters.
1 Dash Orange Bitters.
⅓ Jigger French Vermouth.
⅔ Jigger Dry Gin.
Shake.

OJEN OR SPANISH ABSINTHE COCKTAIL

1 Jigger Ojen Absinthe in large glass of ice. Keep dropping Seltzer in glass and stir with spoon until the outside of glass is frozen and your cocktail is finished. Then add a few drops of Angostura Bitters and strain into a Cocktail glass.

OLD FASHION COCKTAIL

1 Dash Angostura Bitters.
2 Dashes Orange Bitters.
Piece of Cut Loaf Sugar.
Dissolve in two spoonfuls of water.
1 Jigger Liqueur as desired.
Serve in old fashioned glass.

OLIVETTE COCKTAIL

3 Dashes Orange Bitters.
3 Dashes Absinthe.
1 Dash Syrup.
1 Dash Angostura Bitters.
½ Jigger Dry Gin.
½ Jigger French Vermouth.
Stir well and twist Lemon Peel on top.

OPAL COCKTAIL

½ Jigger French Vermouth.
½ Jigger Dry Gin.
1 Dash Absinthe on top.
Stir.

ORANGE BLOSSOM COCKTAIL

½ Jigger Orange Juice.
½ Jigger Gin.
Shake well.

OYSTER BAY COCKTAIL

½ Jigger White Curacao.
⅓ Jigger Dry Gin.
Shake.

PALMER COCKTAIL

2 Dashes Orange Bitters.
½ Jigger Italian Vermouth.
½ Jigger St. Croix Rum.
Shake.

PALMETTO COCKTAIL

½ Jigger St. Croix Rum.
½ Jigger French Vermouth.
1 Dash Angostura Bitters.
Frappe.

PAN-AMERICAN COCKTAIL

1 Dash Syrup.
1 Dash Lemon Juice.
1 Jigger Rye Whiskey.
Shake.

PARADISE COCKTAIL

⅓ Jigger Gin.
⅔ Jigger Apricot Brandy.
Shake.

PARISIAN COCKTAIL

Juice of one Lime.
1 Jigger Byrrh Wine.
Stir.

PARSON COCKTAIL

Same as Rossington.
Shake.

PEACOCK COCKTAIL

1 Dash Amer Picon.
1 Dash Absinthe.
1 Jigger Brandy.
Shake.

PEBLO COCKTAIL

Pousse Cafe.
Shake and strain.

PERFECT COCKTAIL OR McLANE COCKTAIL

½ Jigger Dry Gin.
⅓ Jigger Italian Vermouth.
⅓ Jigger French Vermouth.
1 Orange Peel.
Shake.

PHEASANT COCKTAIL

½ Jigger Martell Brandy.
½ Jigger Dry Gin.
Shake well.

PHILADELPHIA SPECIAL

Martini with Dash of Curacao.

PICK-ME-UP COCKTAIL

⅓ Jigger Martell Brandy.
⅓ Jigger Italian Vermouth.
⅓ Jigger Absinthe.
Frappe.

PICON COCKTAIL

¼ Jigger Italian Vermouth.
¾ Jigger Amer Picon.
1 Orange Peel.
Shake.

PINE TREE COCKTAIL

⅓ Jigger Italian Vermouth.
⅔ Jigger Gin.
Mint.
Shake.

PING PONG COCKTAIL

½ Jigger Sloe Gin.
½ Jigger Creme Yvette.
3 Dashes Lemon Juice.
Shake well.

PINK LADY COCKTAIL
½ Jigger Lime Juice.
½ Jigger Gin.
½ Jigger Apple Jack.
5 Dashes Grenadine.
Shake well.

PLAZA COCKTAIL
¼ Jigger Italian Vermouth.
¾ Jigger High and Dry Gin.
1 Slice Pineapple.
Shake.

POET'S DREAM COCKTAIL
⅓ Jigger French Vermouth.
⅔ Jigger Dry Gin.
2 Dashes Orange Bitters.
2 Dashes Benedictine.
Stir.

POLO FARM COCKTAIL
⅓ Jigger French Vermouth.
⅔ Jigger Dry Gin.
Stir.
Rinse Cocktail glass with Brandy.

POLO COCKTAIL
⅓ Jigger Grape Fruit Juice.
⅓ Jigger Orange Juice.
⅓ Jigger Booth's Tom Gin.
Shake.
Serve in Claret glass

PORTER OR PAT'S COCKTAIL
½ Jigger Dry Gin.
¼ Jigger French Vermouth.
6 Dashes Italian Vermouth.
1 Dash Curacao.
1 Lemon Peel.
1 Fresh Sprig of Mint.
Stir well.

PRAIRIE COCKTAIL
1 Pony Tom Gin.
1 Egg.
Salt and Pepper.

PRINCE COCKTAIL
⅓ Jigger White Creme de Menthe.
⅓ Jigger Dry Gin.
⅓ Jigger Italian Vermouth.
Shake.

PRINCE HENRY COCKTAIL
1 Dash Orange Bitters.
⅓ Jigger Italian Vermouth.
⅓ Jigger Dry Gin.
⅓ Jigger Creme de Menthe White.
Frappe.

PRINCETON COCKTAIL
Gin Cocktail with one squirt Seltzer on top.

RACQUET CLUB COCKTAIL
½ Jigger French Vermouth.
½ Jigger Dry Gin.
Orange Peel on top.

REIS COCKTAIL
2 Dashes Angostura.
2 Dashes Absinthe.
1 Jigger Old Tom Gin.
Shake.

RICHMOND COCKTAIL
⅔ Jigger French Vermouth.
⅓ Jigger Italian Vermouth.
1 Dash Curacao.
Shake well.

RIDING CLUB COCKTAIL
1 Jigger Calisaya.
1 Dash Angostura.
3 Drops Acid Phosphate.
Stir.

ROB ROY COCKTAIL

½ Jgger Italian Vermouth.
½ Jigger McCallum's Perfection Scotch
Whiskey.
1 Dash Angostura.
1 Dash Orange Bitters.

ROBERT BURNS COCKTAIL

1 Dash Absinthe.
¼ Jigger Italian Vermouth.
¾ Jigger Irish or Scotch Whiskey.
Shake well.

ROBIN COCKTAIL

3 Dashes Calisaya.
1 Jigger Perfection Scotch Whiskey.
Stir well.
Serve with one Cherry.

ROSE COCKTAIL

⅕ Jigger Orange Juice.
⅕ Jigger Grenadine Syrup.
⅗ Jigger Gin.
Shake well.

ROSSINGTON COCKTAIL

⅓ Jigger Italian Vermouth.
⅔ Jigger Tom Gin.
Orange Peel.
Stir well.

ROYAL SMILE COCKTAIL

½ Jigger Lime Juice.
½ Pony Grenadine Syrup.
½ Jigger French Vermouth.
½ Jigger Apple Brandy.
1 White of Egg.
Shake.
Serve in Claret glass.

RUBY COCKTAIL

1 Dash Grenadine.
1 Barsponful Apple Jack.
¾ Jigger Dry Gin.
Shake well.

RUBY ROYAL COCKTAIL
½ Jigger Sloe Gin.
½ Jigger French Vermouth.
2 Dashes Raspberry.
Frappe.
1 Cherry.

SABATH COCKTAIL
½ Jigger French Brandy.
½ Jigger Port Wine.
1 Egg.
½ Pony Black Coffee.
½ Barspoon Sugar.
Shake and strain into Claret glass and serve.

SALOME COCKTAIL
¼ Jigger Italian Vermouth.
¼ Jigger French Vermouth.
½ Jigger Dry Gin.
2 Dashes Orange Bitters.
Frappe with 3 Celery Leaves.

SANDY McKAY COCKTAIL
1 White of Egg.
1 Jigger Dry Gin.
½ Jigger Italian Vermouth.
½ Jigger Orange Juice.
1 Barspoon Grenadine.
Shake.
Serve in Claret glass.

SARATOGA COCKTAIL
2 Dashes Pineapple Juice.
2 Dashes Maraschino.
1 Dash Orange Bitters.
1 Jigger Brandy.
Shake.

SCHEUER COCKTAIL
½ Jigger Dubonnet.
½ Jigger Italian Vermouth.
Stir.
1 Dash Angostura Bitters.

SHERMAN COCKTAIL
⅓ Italian Vermouth.
⅔ Jigger Rye Whiskey.
1 Dash Absinthe.
Shake.

SHERRY COCKTAIL
1 Jigger Sherry Wine.
1 Dash Orange Bitters.
1 Dash Angostura Bitters.

SILVER COCKTAIL
2 Dashes Orange Bitters.
⅓ Jigger Italian Vermouth.
⅔ Jigger Dry Gin.
2 Dashes Maraschino.
Shake.

SLOME COCKTAIL
⅓ Jigger Bourbon Whiskey.
⅓ Jigger French Brandy.
⅓ Jigger Dubonnet.
Frappe.

SMITH COCKTAIL
½ Jigger Brandy.
½ Jigger Apricot Brandy.
1 Barspoonful Creme de Menthe.
Shake.
1 Dash Absinthe on top.

SOCIETY COCKTAIL
⅓ Jigger Dry Gin.
⅔ Jigger French Vermouth.
1 Dash Grenadine Syrup.
Shake.

SODA COCKTAIL
3 Dashes Angostura Bitters.
Peel of whole Lemon.
1 Pint Lemon Soda.
Use large glass and lump ice.
Add a teaspoonful of powdered sugar.
Serve.

SOUL KISS NO. 3 COCKTAIL
⅓ Jigger Rye Whiskey.
⅓ Jigger Dubonnet.
⅓ Jigger French Vermouth.
1 Barspoon Orange Juice.
Shake.

SOUTH AFRICA COCKTAIL
½ Jigger Sherry Wine.
1 Dash Angostura Bitters.
½ Jigger Gin.
3 Drops Lime Juice.

SPAULDING COCKTAIL
¼ Jigger Dubonnet.
⅔ Jigger Dry Gin.
1 Barspoon Scotch Whiskey.
Frappe.

SPHINX COCKTAIL
⅔ Jigger High and Dry Gin.
⅙ Jigger Italian Vermouth.
⅙ Jigger French Vermouth.
Very thin slice Lemon Peel on top.
Peel.

ST. FRANCIS COCKTAIL
½ Jigger French Vermouth.
½ Jigger Dry Gin.
1 Pinola.

ST. JOHN COCKTAIL
Old Fashion Martini made of Tom Gin.

ST. PETER COCKTAIL
1 Jigger Dry Gin.
1 Dash Lime Juice.
1 Dash Syrup.
Shake.

STAR COCKTAIL

1 Dash Orange Bitters.
½ Jigger Apple Jack.
½ Jigger Italian Vermouth.
Stir.
Lemon Peel.

STAR COCKTAIL—Old Fashion

1 Barspoonful of Sugar.
1 Dash of Orange Bitters.
⅔ Jigger Apple Jack.
⅛ Jigger Italian Vermouth.
Slice Orange.
Sprig of Mint.

STORY COCKTAIL

½ Jigger Boonekamp Bitters.
½ Jigger Good French Brandy.
Frappe.

STRAWBERRY COCKTAIL

2 Dashes Orange Bitters.
¼ Jigger Strawberry Syrup or Juice of
three Strawberries.
1 Dash Maraschino.
1 Jigger Martell Brandy.
Shake.

SUNSHINE COCKTAIL

(For Two.)

Juice of one Lime.
½ Jigger French Vermouth.
1½ Jigger Tom Gin.
1 Barspoon Grenadine.
1 White of Egg for each one.
Frappe.
Serve in Claret glass.

SWAN COCKTAIL

3 Drops Lime Juice.
2 Drops Angostura Bitters.
½ Jigger French Vermouth.
½ Jigger Dry Gin.
Stir.

TAXI COCKTAIL

½ Jigger French Vermouth.
½ Jigger Dry Gin.
2 Barspoonfuls Lime Juice.
2 Barspoonfuls Absinthe.
Frappe.

THE FAVORITE COCKTAIL

Juice of one Lime.
3 or 4 Sprigs of Mint crushed.
1 Jigger Dry Gin.
1 Pt. Schweppes Ginger Ale.
Fill glass with Cube Ice and serve.

TIP-TOP COCKTAIL

1 Jigger French Vermouth.
4 Dashes Benedictine.
1 Dash Angostura.
3 Dashes Orange Bitters.
Shake.

TREASURY COCKTAIL

⅓ Jigger Italian Vermouth.
⅔ Jigger Dry Gin.
1 Slice of Orange.
Frappe.

TRILBY COCKTAIL

1 Dash Orange Bitters.
⅔ Jigger Tom Gin.
⅙ Jigger French Vermouth.
⅙ Jigger Creme Yvette.
Stir well.
Add 1 Cherry.

TROWBRIDGE COCKTAIL

1 Dash Orange Bitters.
⅔ Jigger French Vermouth.
⅓ Jigger High and Dry Gin.
1 Orange Peel.
Shake well.

TURF COCKTAIL NO. 1

2 Dashes Orange Bitters.
2 Dashes Maraschino.
1 Dash Absinthe.
½ Jigger French Vermouth.
½ Jigger Dry Gin.

TURF COCKTAIL NO. 2

2 Dashes Angostura Bitters.
⅓ Jigger Italian Vermouth.
⅔ Jigger Holland Gin.
Stir.

TUSSETTO COCKTAIL

⅓ Jigger Sherry Wine.
⅔ Jigger Dry Gin.
2 Dashes Orange Bitters.
Stir.

TUXEDO COCKTAIL

1 Dash Maraschino.
3 Dashes Angostura Bitters.
1 Dash Absinthe.
⅔ Jigger Dry Gin.
⅓ Jigger French Vermouth.
1 Barspoon of Sherry Wine.
Stir well.

TWO-SPOT COCKTAIL

½ Jigger French Brandy.
½ Jigger Brown Curacao.
Shake.
Strain into Cocktail glass.
Twist a piece of Lemon Peel on top.

U. C. COCKTAIL

½ Jigger French Vermouth.
½ Jigger Dry Gin.
1 Dash Absinthe.
Shake.

UNION LEAGUE COCKTAIL

1 Dash Orange Bitters.
⅓ Jigger Port Wine.
⅔ Jigger Tom Gin.
Stir well.

VAN WYCK COCKTAIL

½ Jigger Sloe Gin.
½ Jigger Dry Gin.
2 Dashes Orange Bitters.
Shake well.

VAN ZANDT COCKTAIL

1 Dash Apricot Brandy.
½ Jigger French Vermouth.
½ Jigger Dry Gin.
Stir.

VIENNA COCKTAIL

½ Jigger Italian Vermouth.
½ Jigger French Vermouth.
1 Dash Absinthe.
Frappe.

VIRGIN COCKTAIL

½ Jigger High and Dry Gin
½ Jigger Italian Vermouth.
2 Dashes Raspberry Syrup.
2 Dashes Angostura Bitters.
Shake

WALDORF COCKTAIL

⅓ Jigger Rye Whiskey.
⅓ Jigger Italian Vermouth.
⅓ Jigger Absinthe.
2 Dashes Orange Bitters.
Shake.

WALDORF SPECIAL

Juice of one Lime.
1 Jigger Apricotine.
Shake thoroughy and serve in Cocktail glass.

WALDORF QUEEN'S

2 Slices Pineapple moddled.
½ Jigger Dry Gin.
¼ Jigger French Vermouth.
¼ Jigger Italian Vermouth.
Small Piece of Orange.
Frappe well.
Strain into Cocktail glass and serve.

WAXEN COCKTAIL
½ Jigger Italian Vermouth.
½ Jigger Apple Brandy.
⅓ Pony Yellow Chartreuse.
½ Jigger Tom Gin.

WEST INDIA COCKTAIL

2 Dashes Angostura Bitters.
½ Jigger French Vermouth.
2 Lemon Peels.
Shake.

WHITE ELEPHANT COCKTAIL
⅓ Jigger Italian Vermouth.
⅔ Jigger Dry Gin.
White of Egg.
Shake well.

WHITE LION COCKTAIL

1 Barspoon Sugar.
½ Jigger Lemon Juice
3 Dashes Angostura Bitters.
3 Dashes Raspberry Syrup.
1 Jigger St. Croix Rum.
Shake well.

WHITE RAT COCKTAIL
¾ Jigger Absinthe.
¼ Jigger Anisette.
Shake well.

WHITE SLAVE COCKTAIL

1 Jigger Gin.
1 Barspoon Anisette.
1 White of Egg.
2 Barspoons Cream.
Shake.

WHISKEY COCKTAIL

2 Dashes Angostura Bitters.
1 Small Lump of Sugar.
1 Jigger Green River Whiskey.
Piece of Lemon Peel.

WONDER COCKTAIL
⅓ Jigger Italian Vermouth.
⅔ Jigger Dry Gin.
1 Piece Pineapple.
Frappe.

YALE COCKTAIL
1 Dash Orange Bitters.
1 Dash Absinthe.
1 Jigger Tom Gin.
1 Lemon Peel.
Shake.

YANKEE PRINCE COCKTAIL
1 Barspoon Orange Juice.
¼ Jigger Grand Marnier.
¾ Jigger Dry Gin.
1 Filbert Nut.
Frappe.

YORK COCKTAIL
2 Dashes Orange Bitters.
½ Jigger French Vermouth.
½ Jigger McCallum's Perfection Scotch Whiskey.
Frappe.

ZABRISKIE COCKTAIL
1 Dash Orange Bitters.
1 Dash Maraschino.
1 Dash Angostura Bitters.
⅔ Jigger Dry Gin.
⅓ Jigger Italian Vermouth.
Stir well.

ZAZARAC COCKTAIL
Old Fashion Glass.
½ Lump Sugar.
1 Dash Angostura Bitters.
1 Dash Orange Bitters.
1 Dash Anisette.
1 Jigger Bourbon or Rye Whiskey.
Twist Lemon Peel on top.
Add 2 Dashes of Absinthe.
Serve in tall glass.

ZAZA COCKTAIL

½ Jigger Dry Gin.
½ Jigger Dubonnet.
1 Dash Angostura Bitters.

🐞 🐞 🐞

COLLINS

JOHN COLLINS.

Same as Tom Collins except use:
Holland Gin for John Collins.
Brandy for Brandy Collins.
Bourbon or Rye Whiskey for
Bourbon or Rye Collins.
Scotch for Scotch Collins.
Irish Whiskey for Irish Collins.
Rum for Rum Collins.

TOM COLLINS.

Fill Goblet with fine ice.
Juice one small lemon.
One Spoon Powdered Sugar.
One Jigger Dry Gin.
Shake well.
Strain into large thin glass and fill with
one bottle Club Soda or Domestic Soda.
Stir with spoon.

———

No mixed drink is perfect unless ingredients used
are perfect.

COOLERS

Serve in tall glass always.

ARDSLEY COOLER

1 Lump of Ice.
1 Jigger Tom Gin
1 Pint Schweppes Ginger Ale.
1 Large Bunch of Mint.
Serve in Collins Glass.

AUTOMOBILE COOLER

1 Jigger Gin.
1 Pint Schweppes Ginger Ale.
1 Bunch of Mint.
1 Large piece of Ice.

BILLY TAYLOR COOLER

1 Jigger Gin.
Juice of ½ Lime.
1 Pint Club Soda.
1 Cube Ice.

BLACKSTONE COOLER

1 Lemon Rind.
1 Jigger Jamaica Rum.
1 Pint Schweppes Soda.

BULL DOG COOLER

1 Rind of Orange.
Juice of 1 Orange.
1 Lump of Ice in Collins Glass.
1 Jigger Dry Gin.
1 Pint Schweppes Ginger Ale.

BULL PUP COOLER

Juice of ½ a Lemon.
1 Jigger Gin.
1 Pint Schweppes Ginger Ale.
Serve in Collins Glass.
1 Lump of cube ice.

BOSTON COOLER

Juice of ½ a Lemon.
1 Barspoon of Sugar.
1 Jigger Rum.
1 Pint Club Soda.

COUNTRY CLUB COOLER

½ Jigger Grenadine Syrup.
½ Jigger French Vermouth.
1 Pint Club Soda.
1 Lump of cube ice.

DUNHAM COOLER

Peel of an orange in one long string in a Collins glass, with the end hanging over edge of glass.
1 Jigger Orange Juice.
1 Jigger Rye or Bourbon Whiskey.
1 Pint Schweppes Ginger Ale.
1 Piece cube ice.
Stir slowly.

DURKEE COOLER

1 Lemon moddled.
1 Barspoonful Powdered Sugar.
1 Jigger Jamaica Rum.
1 Pint Club Soda.

FLORADORA COOLER

Juice of ½ a Lime.
¼ Jigger Raspberry.
¼ Jigger Dry Gin.
1 Lump cube ice.
1 Pint Schweppes Ginger Ale.

FLORADORA—IMPERIAL STYLE
Juice ½ a Lime.
1 Jigger Brandy.
1 Pint Ginger Ale.

GINGER ALE COOLER
1 Lemon Rind on a spiral shaped piece.
Place a round piece of ice inside of the rind.
Add 1 Pint of Imported Ginger Ale.

GRAPE JUICE COOLER
1 Lemon Rind.
½ Split White or Red Grape Juice.
1 Lump of Ice.
1 Pint Schweppes Soda.

HAWAII COOLER
Rind and Juice of 1 Orange.
1 Jigger Rye.
1 Pint Schweppes Ginger Ale.

HILLY CROFT COOLER
1 Lemon Rind.
1 Lump of Ice.
1 Jigger Tom Gin.
1 Pint Schweppes Ginger Ale.

IRISH WHISKEY COOLER
1 Lemon Rind.
1 Jigger Irish Whiskey.
1 Pint Club Soda.
1 Dash Angostura Bitters.

KHATURA COOLER
¼ Jigger French Vermouth.
¼ Jigger Italian Vermouth.
½ Jigger Gin.
2 Dashes Angostura Bitters.
1 Pint Club Soda.

MINT COOLER
1 Bunch of Fresh Mint.
Crush lightly.
1 Lump Ice.
1 Pint Imported Ginger Ale.

MORAINE COOLER
2 Jiggers Rhine Wine.
½ Lemon moddled.
1 Lemon Rind.
1 Lump of Ice.
⅓ Jigger Curacao.
1 Pint Club Soda.

NARAGANSETT COOLER
1 Rind and Juice of 1 Orange.
1 Jigger Bourbon Whiskey.
1 Pint Schweppes Ginger Ale.

ORANGE BLOSSOM COOLER
2 Jiggers Orange Juice.
1 Jigger Gin.
1 Small Barspoon Sugar.
Collins Glass.
Fine Ice.
Dress with fruit.
Fill glass with Seltzer.

REMSEN COOLER
1 Lemon Rind.
1 Jigger Dry Gin.
1 Pint Club Soda.

ROBERT E. LEE COOLER
1 Dash Absinthe.
Juice ½ Lime.
1 Jigger Scotch Whiskey.
1 Pint Imported Ginger Ale.

SABATH COOLER
½ Jigger Brandy.
½ Jigger Vermouth.
Juice ½ Lime.
1 Pint Club Soda with 2 or 3 Sprigs of Mint on top.

SARSAPARILLA COOLER

3 or 4 Round Slices of Lime.
Juice of ½ Lime.
1 Large Piece of Ice.
1 Pint Schweppes Sarsaparilla.

SCOTCH COOLER

1 Lemon Rind.
3 Large Lumps of Ice in Collins Glass
1 Jigger Scotch Whiskey.
1 Pint Schweppes Soda.

SEA SIDE COOLER

Juice of 1 Lime.
1 Jigger Grenadine Syrup.
1 Pint Club Soda.

WHITE COOLER

Juice of ½ an Orange.
½ Jigger Scotch Whiskey.
1 Dash Angostura Bitters.
1 Bottle Imported Ginger Ale.
Serve in Collins Glass.

CUPS

ADALOR CUP

1 Fresh Peach perforated with fork.
1 Pint Champagne.

BISHOP'S CUP

Use Quart Glass Pitcher.
½ Jigger Lemon Juice.
1 Jigger Plain Syrup.
1 Jigger Jamaica Rum.
1 Pint of Claret or Red Burgundy.
Dress with Fruit and Mint.

BULL'S EYE CUP

1 Pint Sparkling Cider.
1 Pint Schweppes Ginger Ale.
1 Jigger Brandy.

BURGUNDY CUP

Use large Glass Pitcher, into which put
1 Pony Brandy.
1 Pony Brown Curacoa.
1 Pony Maraschino.
1 Quart Chauvenet Burgundy.
1 Pint Sparkling Water.
1 Long Cube Ice.
Stir well and decorate with
1 Lemon Sliced.
1 Orange Sliced.
5 or 6 pieces of Pineapple.
Maraschino Cherries and
1 Small Bunch of Green Mint on top.

CHAMPAGNE CUP

Use Glass Pitcher.
1 Jigger Martell Brandy.
1 Pony Maraschino.
1 Pony Yellow Chartreuse.
1 Pony Syrup.
1 Large Piece Cube Ice.
1 Quart Pommery Sec Champagne.
1 Pint Sparkling Water.
1 Small Lemon sliced.
1 Orange.
6 Pieces of Pineapple sliced.
2 Thin Slices of Pear or Apple.
Cherries.
1 Bunch Fresh Green Mint.
Stir well and put a little powdered sugar
on top.

CHAMPAGNE CUP NO. 2

Use Large Glass Pitcher.
1 Pony Martell Brandy.
1 Pony White Curacoa.
1 Pony Maraschino.
1 Pony Plain Syrup.
Juice of ½ a Lemon.
1 Quart Champagne.
1 Pint Sparkling Water.
1 Long Cube Ice.
2 Pieces Cucumber Rind.
1 Orange Sliced.
1 Lemon Sliced.
4 or 5 Pieces Fresh Pineapple.
6 Cherries.
1 or 2 Pieces of Sliced Pear.
1 Nice Bunch Green Mint.
Stir well and serve in Delmonico Glass.

Historic Cookbooks of the World

CIDER CUP

Use Large Glass Pitcher, into which put
4 Slices Lemon.
5 Slices Orange.
5 Slices Pineapple.
1 Jigger Brandy.
½ Jigger Curacoa.
½ Jigger Maraschino.
1 Quart Champagne Cider
or Sweet Cider, as preferred.
2 Dashes Lemon Juice.
Cherries.
1 Large Piece of Ice.
1 Bunch of Mint on top.

CLARET CUP

Use Large Glass Pitcher, into which put
1 Lemon Sliced.
1 Orange Sliced.
5 Pieces of Fresh Sliced Pineapple.
1 Jigger Curacoa.
1 Jigger Brandy.
1 Jigger Syrup.
1 Dash Maraschino.
1 Dash Lemon Juice.
6 or 8 Maraschino Cherries.
1 Quart B. & G. Claret.
1 Pint Soda or any kind of good Sparkling water and one bunch of Mint on top.

CIDER CUP—Without Liquor

Use Large Glass Pitcher.
Juice of 2 Lemons or Limes.
Juice of 1 Orange.
1 Jigger Grenadine Syrup.
1 Jigger of Plain Syrup.
1 Large Piece of Cube Ice.
3 or 4 Slices of Lemon.
4 Slices of Orange.
4 Slices of Pineapple.
2 Pieces of Cucumber Rind.
½ Dozen Cherries.

(Continued)

CIDER CUP—Without Liquor—Cont'd

1 Quart Champagne Cider.
Stir well with long spoon.
1 Bunch of Mint on top.
Serve in Delmonico Glass.

GINGER ALE—Without Liquor

For Party of 6 People. Glass Pitcher.
Juice of 3 Lemons.
Juice of 3 Oranges.
2 Jiggers Grenadine Syrup.
Sugar to Taste.
Frappé and strain into pitcher.
Add 1 Quart Ginger Ale.
1 Long Cube Ice.
Dress with fruit in season and put one
bunch of Mint on top.
Serve in Delmonico glasses.

GINGER ALE CUP—With Liquor

For about six people. Glass Pitcher.
1 Jigger Martell Brandy.
½ Jigger Maraschino.
1 Dash Benedictine.
3 Pints Schweppes Ginger Ale.
1 Long Cube Ice.
4 or 5 Pieces of Sliced Orange.
4 or 5 Pieces of Sliced Pineapple.
4 or 5 Pieces of Sliced Lemon.
1 Dash Lemon Juice.
1 Bunch of Mint.
Stir well and put little powdered sugar
on top.
Serve in thin glasses.

GRAPE JUICE CUP—Without Liquor.

Juice of 2 Lemons.
Juice of 2 Oranges.
2 Jiggers Grenadine Syrup.
Frappé and strain into Glass Pitcher.
1 Long Cube Ice.
1 Quart White or Red Grape Juice.
1 Pint Apollinaris.
Sugar to taste.
Dress with Fruit and Mint.
Stir well with long spoon.

GRAPE JUICE CUP—With Liquor

For 6 People.   Use Glass Pitcher.
1 Pony Brandy.
1 Pony Maraschino.
1 Pony Yellow Chartreuse.
1 Dash Grenadine Syrup.
Juice of ½ a Lemon.
1 Long Cube Ice.
1 Quart Grape Juice.
1 Pint Apollinaris.
Dress with Fruit and Mint.

LORD LATOUNNE CUP

Use Glass Pitcher.
1 Lemon Rind cut thin.
2 Jiggers Sherry.
1 Sprig Mint.
½ Dozen Maraschino Cherries.
1 Quart Claret.
1 Pint Schweppes Soda.
Stir well and serve in Delmonico Glass.

MOSELLE WINE CUP

1 Pony Martell Cognac.
1 Pony Maraschino.
1 Dash Yellow Chartreuse.

(Continued)

MOSELLE WINE CUP—Cont'd

    1 Dash Benedictine.
    1 Quart Moselle Wine.
    1 Pint Apollinaris.
    1 Large, Long Cube Ice.
    6 or 8 Cherries or Grapes.
    1 Lemon Sliced.
    1 Orange Sliced.
    2 or 3 Pieces of Pineapple.
    1 Bunch of Green Mint.
    Stir well and serve in Delmonico Glasses

RHINE WINE CUP

    Use Large Glass Pitcher.
    1 Jigger French Brandy.
    ½ Jigger Maraschino.
    ½ Jigger Benedictine.
    1 Dash White Curacao.
    1 Long Cube Ice.
    1 Pint Apollinaris.
    1 Quart Rhine Wine.
    4 Pieces Sliced Lemon.
    6 Pieces Sliced Orange.
    6 Pieces Sliced Pineapple.
    2 Pieces Sliced Pear.
    6 or 8 Maraschino Cherries.
    1 Dash Lemon Juice.
    Stir well and decorate with
    1 Bunch Fresh Mint.

SAUTERNES CUP

    Use Large Glass Pitcher.
    1 Pony French Brandy.
    1 Pony Yellow Chartreuse.
    1 Pony Maraschino (French).
    1 Long Cube Ice.
    1 Pint Apollinaris.
    1 Quart Sauternes.
    1 Pony Curacao.
    Juice of ½ a Lemon.
    ½ Lemon Sliced Thin.
    4 or 5 Pieces of Sliced Orange.
    4 Pieces of Sliced Pineapple.

(Continued)

Historic Cookbooks of the World

SAUTERNES CUP—Cont'd

2 Pieces Cucumber Rind.
6 Maraschino Cherries.
1 Bunch of Green Mint on top.

SAUTERNES CUP—(Southern Style)

Use Large Glass Pitcher.
1 Jigger Lemon Juice.
½ Jigger French Brandy.
½ Jigger Curacao.
½ Jigger Benedictine.
1 Long, Large Cube Ice.
1 Quart Barton & Guestier Sauternes.
½ Lemon Sliced.
½ Orange Sliced.
4 or 5 Slices Pineapple.
Maraschino Cherries.
1 Pint Apollinaris.
Stir well and put 1 Bunch of Green Mint on top.
Serve in Delmonico Glass.

TURK'S NECK CUP

1 Pint Pommery Champagne.
1 Pint Champagne.
1 Pint Claret.
1 Long Cube Ice.
Dress with Fruit and Mint.

VELVET CUP

Use Glass Pitcher.
1 Pint Champagne.
1 Pint Stout.
1 Long Cube Ice.
Dark Imported Beer may be used in place of Stout if preferred.

DAISYS

BRANDY DAISY
Juice of ½ a Lemon.
Juice of ½ a Lime.
½ Jigger Raspberry Syrup.
1 Jigger Brandy in Goblet.
Fine Ice.
Fruit.

CHOCOLATE DAISY
Juice of 1 Lime.
½ Jigger Brandy.
½ Jigger Port.
⅓ Jigger Raspberry Syrup.
Goblet.
Fine Ice.
Fruit.

GIN DAISY
Juice ½ Lemon.
1 Jigger Gin.
½ Jigger Raspberry Syrup.
In Goblet Fine Ice.
Fruits.

GINGER DAISY
Juice ½ Lime.
½ Barspoonful Sugar.
½ Jigger Gin.
½ Jigger Brandy.
Shake in Fine Ice.
Pour into Goblet.
Decorate with Fruits and Mint.

HIGHLAND DAISY
Juice ½ Lemon.
Juice ½ Lime.
Juice ½ Orange.
¾ Jigger McCallum's Scotch Whiskey.
1 Jigger Syrup.
In Goblet Fine Ice.
Decorate with Fruit.

JUNE DAISY

Juice ½ Lemon.
Juice ½ Lime.
Juice ½ Orange.
½ Jigger Raspberry Syrup.
In Goblet Fine Ice.
Fill with Ginger Ale.
Decorate with Fruit.

RUM DAISY

Juice ½ Lemon.
1 Jigger Rum.
½ Jigger Raspberry Syrup.
In Goblet with Fine Ice.
Decorate with Fruit.

STAR DAISY

Juice ½ Lime.
½ Jigger Gin.
½ Jigger Apple Jack.
½ Jigger Grenadine Syrup.
In Goblet Fine Ice.
Fruits.

WHISKEY DAISY

Juice ½ Lemon.
1 Jigger Whiskey.
½ Jigger Raspberry Syrup.
In Goblet with Fine Ice.
Fruits.

EGGNOGS

BRANDY EGGNOG

1 Egg.
1 Jigger Brandy.
1 Dash Jamaica Rum.
1 Barspoonful Sugar.
Milk, shake, strain.
Dash of Nutmeg on top.

RUM EGGNOG

1 Jigger Jamaica Rum
1 Barspoonful Sugar.
1 Egg.
Milk.
Shake and strain.
Dash of Nutmeg on top.

WHISKEY EGGNOG

1 Jigger Bourbon.
1 Dash Jamaica Rum.
1 Egg.
1 Barsponful Sugar.
Milk.
Shake and strain.
Dash of Nutmeg on top.

No mixed drink is perfect unless ingredients used are perfect.

FIZZES

AMER PICON POUFFLE FIZZ

1 Jigger Amer Picon.
1 Pony Grenadine Syrup.
1 White of Egg.
Shake, strain and fill glass with Siphon.

ANGOSTURA FIZZ

Juice of one-half a Lemon.
1 Barspoonful Sugar.
½ Jigger Angostura.
1 White of Egg.
1 Barspoonful of Cream.
Shake well and strain into Fizz glass.
Fill with Siphon.

BAYARD FIZZ

Juice of 1½ Lemons.
1 Barspoon of Sugar.
1 Jigger Dry Gin.
1 Dash Maraschino.
1 Dash Raspberry Syrup.
Shake, strain and fill glass with Siphon.

BIRD OF PARADISE FIZZ

Same as Silver Fizz.
Add 1 dash of Raspberry Syrup.

BISMARCK FIZZ

Juice of one-half a Lemon.
1 Barspoonful Sugar.
1 Egg.
1 Jigger Sloe Gin.
Fill glass with siphon.
Shake.

BRANDY FIZZ

Juice of one Lemon.
1 Barspoonful of Sugar.
1 Jigger French Brandy.
Shake and strain.
Fill glass with Siphon.
2 Dashes Yelow Chartreuse.

CANADIAN WHISKEY FIZZ

Juice of one-half a Lemon.
1 Barspoonful Sugar.
1 Jigger Canadian Whiskey.
Shake. strain and fill glass with Siphon.

CANADIAN FIZZ

Juice of one Lime.
1 Barspoonful of Sugar.
1 Jigger Gin.
1 Egg.
Shake well, strain and fill gass with
Siphon.

CHICAGO FIZZ

Juice of one-half a Lemon.
1 Barspoonful of Sugar.
½ Jigger Jamaica Rum.
½ Jigger Port Wine.
1 White of Egg.
Shake, strain.
Fill glass with Siphon.

CLARET FIZZ

Juice of one-haf a Lemon.
1 Barspoonful Sugar.
1 Glass Claret.
Shake and strain.
Fill glass with Siphon.

DAISY FIZZ

Juice of one-half a Lemon.
Juice of one -half a Lime.
½ Jigger Orange Juice.
⅔ Jigger Brandy.
Shake, strain and fill glass with Siphon.

DIAMOND FIZZ

Same as Gin Fizz.
Fill glass with Paul Garrett Champagne
and serve.

ELSIE FERGUSON FIZZ

½ a Lemon Crushed.
2 Strawberries Crushed.
1 Jigger High and Dry Gin.
2 Barspoonfuls Grenadine Syrup.
4 Barspoonfuls Cream.
Shake well, strain into Fizz glass and
fill with Siphon.

GALVEZ FIZZ

Juice of one Lemon.
1 Barspoonful of Sugar.
4 Dashes Raspberry Syrup.
1 Jigger Dry Gin.
1 White of Egg.
1 Dash Orange Flower Water.
1 Jigger Cream.
Shake very well, strain into Lemonade
glass and fill with Siphon.

GIN FIZZ

Juice of one-haf a Lemon.
1 Barspoon of Sugar.
1 Jigger Gin.
Shake, strain into Fizz glass and fill with
Siphon.

GRENADINE GIN FIZZ

Juice of one-half a Lemon.
⅓ Jigger Grenadine Syrup.
1 Jigger Tom Gin.
Shake well, strain into Fizz glass and
fill with Siphon.

GOLDEN GIN FIZZ

Juice of one-half a Lemon.
1 Barspoonful of Sugar.
1 Jigger of Dry Gin.
1 Yolk of Egg.
Shake well and strain into Lemonade
glass and fill with Fizz water.

HOLLAND GIN FIZZ

Juice of one-half a Lemon.
1 Barspoonful of Sugar.
1 Jigger Holland Gin.
1 Dash White Creme de Menthe.
Shake well and strain into Fizz glass.
Fill glass with Siphon.

IRISH WHISKEY FIZZ

Juice of one-half a Lemon.
1 Barspoonful of Sugar.
1 Jigger Irish Whiskey.
Shake well and strain into Fizz glass.
Fill glass with Siphon.

JAP FIZZ

Juice of one-half a Lemon.
1 Barspoonful of Sugar.
1 White of Egg.
½ Jigger Port Wine.
½ Jigger Rye Whiskey.
Shake well, strain into Fizz glass.
Fill with Siphon.

KING COLE FIZZ

Gin Fizz with Grenadine Syrup.
Frappe.

LALA ROOCK FIZZ

Juice of one-half Lime.
1 Barspoonful of Sugar.
⅓ Jigger Vanilla.
⅓ Jigger Brandy.
⅓ Jigger Jamaica Rum.
1 Barspoonful of Cream.
Shake, strain and fill with Siphon.

MERRY WIDOW FIZZ

Juice of one-half a Lemon.
Juice of one-half an Orange.
1 Barspoonful of Sugar.
1 Jigger Sloe Gin.
1 White of Egg.
Shake well, strain into Lemonade glass.
Fill with Siphon.

MORNING GLORY FIZZ

Juice of one-half a Lemon.
Juice of one-half a Lime.
2 Dashes Absinthe.
1 White of Egg.
1 Jigger Scotch Whiskey.
1 Barspoonful of Sugar.
Shake, strain and fill glass with Siphon.

NEW ORLEANS FIZZ

Juice of one-half a Lemon.
2 Dashes Orange Flower Water.
Small spoon of Granulated Sugar.
1 Jigger Cream.
1 Jigger Dry Gin.
1 White of Egg.
1 Dash of Lime Juice.
Shake well, strain into Lemonade glass
and add Siphon.

REMUS FIZZ

Juice of one-half a Lemon.
1 Dash Grenadine.
1 Dash Lime Juice.
1 Barspoonful Sugar.
1 Jigger Dry Gin.
½ Jigger Fresh Cream.
Shake very well.
Strain into Lemonade glass and fill with
Fizz water.

ROYAL GIN FIZZ

Juice of one-half a Lemon.
1 Barspoonful Sugar.
1 Jigger Gin.
1 White of Egg
Shake, strain and fill with Siphon.

RUEBLI FIZZ

Juice of one-half a Lemon.
Juice of one-half an Orange.
⅓ Jigger Grenadine Syrup.
1 Jigger Rhine Wine.
Shake, strain, fill glass with Siphon.

SCOTCH WHISKEY FIZZ

Juice of one small Lemon.
1 Barspoonful of Sugar.
1 Jigger Perfection Scotch Whiskey.
Shake, strain into glass and fill with Siphon.

SILVER BOWL OR SNOWBALL FIZZ

1 Jigger Grape Fruit Juice.
½ Jigger Dry Gin.
½ Jigger Rhine Wine.
2 Dashes Orange Flower Water.
1 White of Egg.
1 Barspoonful Sugar.
Shake very well and strain.

SILVER FIZZ

Juice of one-half a Lemon.
1 Barspoonful of Sugar.
1 Jigger Dry Gin.
1 White of Egg.
Shake well, strain into Lemonade glass and fill with Siphon.

SUNSHINE FIZZ

Juice of one-half a Lemon.
Juice of one-half an Orange.
1 White of Egg.
1 Jigger Rye Whiskey.
Shake, strain into Lemonade glass and fill with Siphon.

STRAWBERRY FIZZ

Juice of one-half a Lemon.
¼ Spoon Sugar.
½ Dozen Strawberries.
1 Jigger Tom Gin.
Shake, strain and Fizz with Siphon.

VIOLET FIZZ

Juice of one-half a Lemon.
1 Barspoonful Sugar.
¾ Jigger Gin.
¼ Jigger Creme de Violet.
Frappe, strain into Fizz glass and fill with Siphon.

WALDORF FIZZ

Juice of one Orange.
Juice of one Lemon.
1 Egg.
1 Barspoonful Sugar.
Shake, strain and fill glass with Siphon.

WHISKEY FIZZ

Juice of one-half a Lemon.
1 Barspoonful Sugar.
1 Jigger Rye or Bourbon Whiskey.
Whichever customer prefers.
Shake, strain and fill glass with Fizz water.

WHISKEY GRENADINE FIZZ

Juice of one-half a Lemon.
⅓ Jigger Grenadine Syrup.
⅔ Jigger Rye or Bourbon Whiskey.
Shake very well, strain into Fizz glass and fill with Siphon.

TOM GIN FIZZ
DRY GIN FIZZ
SLOE GIN FIZZ

Same as Gin Fizz except substitute Gins in order named.

FLIPS

BRANDY FLIP

1 Jigger Brandy.
1 Barspoonful Sugar.
1 Egg.
Shake well in fine Ice.
Grate Nutmeg on top.

BUSSE FLIP

1 Jigger Sloe Gin.
1 Yolk of Egg.
2 Dashes Apricot Brandy.
½ Barspoonful of Sugar.
Shake well in fine Ice.
Strain into Claret glass.
Grated Nutmeg on top.

COFFEE FLIP

½ Jigger Brandy.
½ Jigger Port.
1 Egg.
1 Barspoonful of Sugar.
Shake well.
Grated Nutmeg on top.

CHOCOLATE FLIP

½ Jigger Martell Brandy.
½ Jigger Sloe Gin.
1 Yolk of Egg.
1 Barspoonful of Sugar.
Shake well in fine Ice.

CREAM FLIP

1 Egg.
3 Jiggers Cream.
1 Dash Curacao.
Shake well in Fine Ice.
Grated Nutmeg on top.

EGG FLIP

1 Egg.
1 Barspoonful Sugar.
1 Barspoonful Maraschino.
1 Jigger Milk Shake.
Grated Nutmeg on top.

GIN FLIP

1 Jigger Gin.
1 Egg.
1 Barspoonful Sugar.
Shake well and strain.

PORT WINE FLIP

1 Jigger Port.
1 Egg.
1 Barspoonful Sugar.
Shake, strain.
Grated Nutmeg on top.

REVIVER FLIP

1 Jigger Sloe Gin.
¼ Jigger Curacao.
1 Egg.
Shake well.
Grated Nutmeg on top.

RUM FLIP

1 Jigger Jamaica Rum.
1 Egg.
1 Barspoonful Sugar.
Shake well, strain.
Grated Nutmeg on top.

SHERRY FLIP

1 Jigger Sherry.
1 Egg.
1 Barspoonful Sugar.
Shake.
Strain.
Grated Nutmeg top.

FRAPPES

ABSINTHE FRAPPE
½ Jigger Absinthe, Green.
½ Jigger Water.
Shake well in Fine Ice.

FRAPPES ASSORTED
Fill cocktail glass with fine shaved ice
and fill with any Cordial customer may
ask for as
Creme de Menthe Frappé.
Curacao Frappé.
Chartreuse Frappé.
Benedictine Frappé.
Anisette Frappé, etc.

HIGH BALLS

AMER PICON HIGH BALL
1 Jigger Amer Picon.
¼ Jigger Grenadine.
1 lump Ice.
Fill with Siphon.

BERMUDA HIGH BALL
⅓ Jigger Brandy.
⅓ Jigger Gin.
⅓ Jigger French Vermouth.
1 lump Ice.
Fill with Siphon.

BOURBON HIGH BALL
1 Jigger Bourbon.
1 lump Ice.
Fill with Siphon.

BRANDY HIGH BALL
1 Jigger Brandy.
1 lump Ice.
Fill with Siphon.

CASCADE HIGH BALL
½ Jigger Italian Vermouth.
½ Jigger Creme de Cassis.
1 lump Ice.
Fill with Siphon.

GIN HIGH BALL
1 Jigger Gin.
1 lump Ice.
1 Lemon Peel.
Fill with Siphon.

IRISH ROSE HIGH BALL
1 Jigger Irish Whiskey.
⅓ Jigger Grenadine Syrup.
·1 lump Ice.
Fill with Siphon.
Stir.

PALL MALL HIGH BALL

⅓ Jigger Brandy.
⅓ Jigger Italian Vermouth.
⅓ Jigger Gin.
1 lump Ice.
Fill with Siphon.

POMPIER

½ Jigger French Vermouth.
½ Jigger Creme de Cassis.
1 lump Ice.
Fill with Siphon.

RYE HIGH BALL

1 Jigger Rye.
1 lump Ice.
Fill with Siphon.

SCOTCH HIGH BALL

1 Jigger McCallum's Perfection Scotch
Whiskey.
1 lump Ice.
Fill with Seltzer.

QUEEN'S HIGH BALL

⅔ Jigger Amer Picon.
1 Pony Grenadine Syrup.
1 Clear Piece Ice in Glass.
Fill Glass with Siphon.
Serve.

HOT DRINKS

AMERICAN GROG

1 Lump Sugar.
½ Lemon Juice.
1 Jigger Jamaica Rum.
Fill Glass with Hot Water.

BLUE BLAZER

Use heavy bar glasses or metal mugs.
½ Lump Sugar.
Fill Glass ⅔ full Hot Water.
Float with Scotch or Rye.
Set the liquid on fire and pour from one glass to another 3 or 4 times.
Twist Lemon on top and serve.

BURNT BRANDY WITH PEACH

Burn 1 Jigger Brandy with 1 Lump Sugar in a saucer.
Place 2 Slices Dried Peach in Hot Toddy Glass.
Pour liquid over the peach.

CAFE BOULES

Rub edge of Cocktail glass with a Lemon Peel all around.
Dip in powdered Sugar.
Fill ⅞ Hot Coffee, ⅛ Brandy.
Light witch match and serve.

CLARET PUNCH, HOT

½ Lump Sugar.
Fill glass ⅔ Hot Water.
Fill with French Claret.
1 Lemon Peel.

COLUMBIA SKIN

½ Lump Sugar.
1 Jigger Rye Whiskey.
1 Lemon Peel.
Fill with Hot Water.

HOT AMERICAN GROG

½ Lump Sugar.
1 Jigger Jamaica Rum.
Fill with Hot Water.
1 Slice Lemon.

HOT APPLEJACK TODDY

½ Lump Sugar.
1 Jigger Apple Brandy in Hot Toddy
Glass. Fill with Hot Water.
1 Lemon Peel.

HOT CREOLE PUNCH

2 Barspoonfuls Syrup.
2 Dashes Jamaica Rum.
1 Dash Hungarian Apricot Brandy.
1 Jigger French Claret.
1 Barspoon Spices.
Lemon Peel.
Have this heated on stove till nearly
boiling.

HOT LEMONADE

1 Lemon Juice.
1 Tablespoon Sugar.
Fill with Hot Water.
1 Slice Lemon.

HOT MILK PUNCH

1 Jigger Brandy or Whiskey.
2 Barspoonfuls Sugar.
1 Dash Jamaica Rum.
Fill with Hot Milk.
Stir and Serve.

HOT SPICED RUM

¼ Lump Sugar.
1 Jigger Rum.
½ Barspoonful Allspice.
Fill with Hot Water.

MULL CLARET

    1 Lump Sugar.
    2 Dashes Lemon Juice.
    1 Dash Angostura Bitters.
    2 Jiggers Claret.
    1 Barspoon Mixed Spices.
    Heat Poker red hot and stick in liquid
    till boiling and serve.

PORT WINE NEGUS

    ½ Lump Sugar.
    Fill glass ⅔ Hot Water.
    1 Jigger Port Wine.
    Stir.
    Grated Nutmeg on top.

JULEPS

BRANDY JULEP

    2 Barspoonfuls Syrup.
    1 Jigger Brandy in Silver Cup filled with
    Crushed Ice.
    Stir gently.
    Set large bunch of Mint on top.
    Serve with straws.

GIN JULEP

    2 Barspoonfuls Syrup.
    1 Jigger Gin in Silver Cup.
    Crushed Ice.
    Stir.
    Bunch of Mint on top.
    Serve with Straws.

GRAPE JUICE

    1 Barspoonful Syrup.
    ½ Split Grape Juice in Silver Cup.
    Stir.
    Large Bunch of Mint on top.
    Serve with Straws.

PINEAPPLE JULEP

Juice of two Oranges.
1 Jigger Raspberry Syrup.
1 Jigger Maraschino.
1 Jigger Tom Gin.
1 Quart Moselle.
1 Sliced Pineapple.
Ice and serve with Straws.

KENTUCKY MINT JULEP

Two Barspoons Syrup.
1 Jigger Green River Bourbon in Silver
Cup filled with Crushed Ice.
Stir gently, then take ice pick and from
a big chunk of ice chop off Fine Ice so it
will adhere to side of cup. Carefully
place a nice, large bunch of Kentucky
Mint on top and serve with straws.

MINT JULEP, WESTERN STYLE

In Julep Cup or Lemonade Glass crush
1 Lump of Sugar and 3 Sprigs of Mint.
Fill with Fine Ice.
1 Jigger Green River Bourbon.
½ Barspoonful Jamaica Rum.
Stir well.
Decorate with Fruits.
Place a bunch of Mint on top.
Serve with Straws.

No mixed drink is perfect unless ingredients used
are perfect.

LEMONADES

ANGOSTURA LEMONADE
Add 1 Teaspoon Angostura Bitters to each Glass of Lemonade.

APOLLINARIS
Juice of one Lemon.
1 Tablespoonful Sugar.
1 Split Apollinaris.
Stir well.
Decorate with Fruits.
Serve with Straws.

CLARET LEMONADE
Plain Lemonade.
Float Claret on top.

CLUB SODA LEMONADE
1 Tablespoonful Sugar.
Juice of one Lemon.
1 Split Club soda.
Stir.
Decorate with Fruits.

EGG LEMONADE
Juice one Lemon.
1 Tablespoonful Sugar.
1 Egg.
Fill with fine Ice and Water.
Shake well.

FRUIT LEMONADE
Plain Lemonade.
Add Slices Pineapple, Oranges, Cherries and other fruit in season.

HOT LEMONADE
1 Tablespoonful Sugar.
Juice one Lemon.
Fill with Hot Water.
Stir.
Add Slice of Lemon.

ORANGEADE
Juice one Orange.
Juice one-half Lemon.
½ Tablespoonful Sugar.
Fill Glass with Ice and Water
Shake well.
Decorate with Fruits.

PLAIN LEMONADE
Juice of one Lemon.
1 Tablespoonful Sugar.
Fill with Fine Ice and Distilled Water.
Decorate with Fruits and serve.

SELTZER LEMONADE
Juice one Lemon.
One Tablespoonful Sugar.
Fill Glass one-half full Ice.
Fill with Seltzer.
Stir.
Decorate with Fruits.

SODA LEMONADE
Juice one Lemon.
One Tablespoonful Sugar.
Fill Glass one-half full Ice.
Add one pint Lemon or Plain Soda.
Stir gently.
Decorate with Fruits.

WHISKEY LEMONADE
Plain Lemonade.
Float one Jigger Whiskey on top.
Fruits.

MISCELLANEOUS

ABSINTHE DRIP

1 Pony Absinthe in large Glass.
Fill Drip Glass with Fine Ice and a Jig-
ger of plain Water.
Let drip into Absinthe, then pour into
Iced Glass.

ALE SANGAREE

Fill Glass with Ale.
1 Barspoonful Powdered Sugar.
Stir gently.
Grated Nutmeg on top.

AMER PICON POUFFLE

¾ Jigger Amer Picon.
¼ Jigger Grenadine Syrup.
1 White of Egg.
Shake, strain and fill glass with Siphon.

AMMONIA AND SELTZER

About ten dops of Spirits of Ammonia
Aromatic.   Put into a small glass of
Seltzer.
Stir well.

ANGEL BLUSH

¼ Maraschino.
¼ Creme Yvette.
¼ Benedictine.
¼ Cream on top.

ANGEL DREAM

⅓ Maraschino.
⅓ Creme Yvette.
⅓ Cream on top.

ANGEL KISS
⅔ Benedictine.
¼ Cream on top.

ANGEL TIP
¾ Maraschino.
¼ Cream on top.

ANGOSTURA PHOSPHATE
Use a Phosphate Glass.
½ Teaspoonful Acid Phosphate.
1 Teaspoonful Angostura Bitters.
2 Tablespoonfuls Lemon Syrup, or Juice
of ½ Lemon well sweetened.
Fill Glass with Carbonic Water.

ANGOSTURA GINGER ALE
1 Glass Ginger Ale.
3 Dashes Angostura Bitters.

ANGOSTURA SODA
Large Bar Glass with two or three Lumps
of Ice.
5 or 6 Dashes Angostura Bitters.
1 or 2 Slices of Orange.
Fill up glass with Lemon Soda and place
a teaspoon filled with Sugar on top of
the glass for customer to put it in himself.

APPETIZER
Four Dashes Absinthe.
½ Jigger Dry Gin.
½ Jigger French or Italian Vermouth.
Use Delmonico glass and add little
Seltzer.
Shake well.

BACHELOR DREAM
¼ Jigger Curacao.
¼ Jigger Maraschino.
¼ Jigger Creme Violet.
¼ Jigger Whipped Cream on top.

BALTIMORE BRACER

½ Jigger Anisette.
½ Jigger Brandy.
1 White of Egg.
Shake, strain into Delmonico glass.
Fill with Siphon.

BEER SHANDY

½ Glass of Beer.
½ Glass of Ale.

BIRD OF PARADISE

Silver Fizz with little Raspberry Syrup
and two dashes of Angostura Bitters.

BISSELL SWEEPER

Lemonade Glass.
Whiskey Rickey with one split Imported Ginger Ale and fill glass with Siphon.

BISHOP

½ Barspoonful Sugar.
½ Lemon Juice.
½ Orange Juice.
½ Glass Fine Ice.
Fill with Burgundy Wine.
1 Dash Jamaica Rum on top.
Dress with Fruit.

BLACK JACK

¼ Jigger Cold Coffee.
¼ Jigger Brandy.
¼ Jigger Kirschwasser.
Shake well. Rub edge of glass with
Lemon Rind.
Dip in Sugar.

BRADLEY MARTIN

Iced Creme de Menthe with ½ Jigger
Curacao on top.

BRAIN DUSTER

⅛ Jigger Brandy.
⅓ Jigger Dubonnet.
⅓ Jigger French Vermouth.
Shake, strain into Delmonico glass

BRANDY CHAMPRELLE

¼ Jigger Anisette.
¼ Jigger Curacao.
¼ Jigger Kirschwasser.
¼ Jigger Chartreuse.
2 Dashes Angostura Bitters on top.

BRANDY CRUSTA

¼ Jigger Maraschino.
¾ Jigger Brandy.
1 Dash Lemon Juice.
Shake, strain and dress with Fruit.

BRANDY FIX

1 Lime and Juice.
½ Barspoonful Sugar.
1 Pony Pineapple Juice.
2 Dashes Yellow Chartreuse.
⅔ Jigger Brandy.
Shake, strain into Goblet filled with fine Ice.
Decorate with fruit.

BRANDY FLOAT

Fill a pony glass with Brandy. Put a whiskey glass over it, rim down. Reverse the glasses, holding them tightly together so as to keep the Brandy in the pony glass, then fill the whiskey glass one-half full of Seltzer and draw out the pony glass very carefully so as to leave the Brandy floating on top of Seltzer.

BRANDY SCAFFA

¼ Jigger Raspberry Syrup.
¼ Jigger Maraschino.
¼ Jigger Chartreuse.
¼ Jigger Martell Brandy.

BRANDY SANGAREE

1 Barspoonful of Sugar.
¾ Jigger Brandy.
¼ Jigger Port Wine.
Fill glass with Ice.
Shake, strain and serve.

CHOCOLATE CREAM PUFF

3 Dashes Acid Phosphate.
1 Pony Cream.
1 Yolk of one Egg.
Shake, strain and fill glass with Siphon.

CLICQUOT

½ Jigger Orange Juice.
1 Jigger Rye.
2 Dashes St. Croix Rum.
Serve in old fashion glass and twist a
Lemon Peel on top.

COLUMBIA SKIN

Hot Rye Toddy.

CREAM PUFF.

½ Barspoonful Sugar.
1 Jigger Cream.
1 Jigger St. Croix Rum.
Shake, strain and add little Siphon on
top.

CREOLE LADY

¼ Jigger Maraschino.
¾ Jigger Bourbon.
1 Jigger Madeira.
2 Cherries.
Shake, strain into Claret glass.

CRYSTAL SLIPPER

2 Dashes Orange Bitters.
¾ Jigger Dry Gin.
¼ Jigger Creme Yvette.
Shake well.

DE LUXE BRACER

1 Pony White Absinthe.
1 Dash French Vermouth.
1 Dash Anisette.
1 Dash Yellow Chartreuse.
Shake well and strain into Delmonico
Glass. Add a little Seltzer and serve.

DIARRHEA MIXTURE

Use Whiskey glass.
3 Dashes Jamaica Ginger.
1 Dash Peppermint.
1 Pony Blackberry Brandy.
1 Pony good Brandy and put a little Nutmeg on top.

DOG DAYS

1 Jigger Old Vatted Scotch.
1 Pint Ginger Ale.
2 Slices Orange.
Collins Glass.
1 Cube of Ice.

DREAM

½ Lemon Juice.
½ Barspoon Sugar.
1 Jigger Dry Gin.
1 White of Egg.
2 Dashes Assorted Cordials on top.

DUTCH MIKE

½ Lime.
2 Dashes Amer Picon.
1 Jigger Tom Gin.
1 Lump Ice.
Long Glass.
Fill with Seltzer.

EGG PHOSPHATE
1 Egg.
1 Barspoon Sugar.
Juice of one Orange.
3 Dashes Acid Phosphate.
Shake well, strain and serve with straw.

FRAZIE
⅞ Jigger Maraschino Holland.
⅛ Jigger Hungarian Apricot.
Float.

FRENCH FLAG
⅓ Jigger Grenadine
⅓ Jigger Maraschino.
⅓ Creme Yvette.

FLOATER
¾ Russian Kummel.
¼ Good Brandy.
Iced.

GARDEN OF EDEN.
½ Jigger Apricot Brandy.
½ Creme Yvette.

GOLDEN DREAM
½ Lemon Juice.
1 Barspoon Sugar.
1 Yolk of Egg.
1 Jigger Dry Gin.
Shake, strain into Claret glass, little
Seltzer on top.

GOLDEN SLIPPER
Use Sherry glass.
¼ Yellow Chartreuse.
1 Whole Egg.
Fill glass with Eau de Vie de Dantzig.

GOLFER

Use old fashion glass.
Juice of one-half Lime.
1 Jigger McCallum's Perfection Scotch Whiskey.
1 Lump of Ice.
Little Powdered Sugar and fill glass with Seltzer.

GREEN TIE

½ Jigger Creme de Menthe Green.
½ Jigger de Rose.
Float.

HALSTED STREET

Use Glass Pitcher.
1 Pint Paul Garrett Champagne.
1 Pint Beer.
Mixed.

HAPPY THOUGHT

⅙ Jigger Anisette.
⅙ Jigger Creme de Cacao.
⅙ Jigger Creme de Rose.
⅙ Jigger Green Creme de Menthe.
⅙ Jigger Creme Yvette.
⅙ Martell Brandy.

HARVESTER

1 Jigger Orange Juice.
½ Jigger Dry Gin.
Shake in fine ice and strain into a Claret glass.

HEADACHE DRINKS

Take two Lemonade glasses, into one of which put a barspoonful of Bromo Seltzer or Bromo Soda, as preferred.
Fill the other glass half full of water. Pour the water into the bromo, and pour from one glass to the other until thoroughly mixed. Drink at once.

HOOK AND EYE

½ Jigger Brandy.
½ Jigger Apricot Brandy.
1 Barspoonsful of White Creme de Menthe.
1 Dash of Absinthe.
Shake.

HORSE'S NECK

1 Rind of one Lemon cut thin.
1 pint Imported Ginger Ale.
1 Cube of Collins glass.

HUNGARIAN BRACER

Use Whiskey glass.
½ Jigger Italian Vermouth.
½ Jigger Good Rye Whiskey.
2 Dashes Angostura Bitters.
2 Dashes Absinthe.
Twist one Lemon Peel over one small glass Seltzer with one dash Acid Phosphate on the side.

IRISH ROSE

Irish Whiskey High Ball with three or four dashes of Grenadine Syrup.

JERSEY FLASHLIGHT

2 Lumps Sugar.
2 Dashes Angostura Bitters.
1 Jigger Apple Brandy.
Twist Lemon Peel on top.
Add little hot water and light with match and serve.

JERSEY LILY POUSSE CAFE

½ Jigger Green Chartreuse.
½ Jigger Brandy.
10 Drops Angostura Bitters.
Pour Brandy in carefully so it will not mix, and serve.

JERSEY SUNSET

½ Jigger Syrup.
1 Jigger Plain Water.
1 Jigger Apple Brandy.
1 Lemon Peel.
Crushed Ice in the Goblet.
Add two drops of Angostura Bitters
which should not be stirred in, but be
allowed to drop slowly through the above
mixture.

JUNE ROSE

½ Lime Juice.
½ Lemon Juice.
1 Orange Juice.
½ Jigger Dry Gin.
½ Jigger Raspberry Syrup.
Shake, strain, fill glass with Siphon.

KING'S CORDIAL

¾ Maraschino.
¼ Scotch Whiskey. Float.
Cordial Glass.

KNICKERBEIN

½ Jigger Benedictine.
1 Yolk of Egg.
3 Dashes Kummel.
1 Dash Angostura Bitters.
Use Sherry gass and see that different
ingredients are not mixed.

KNICKERBOCKER

¼ Jigger Raspberry Syrup.
Juice of one Lemon.
1 Jigger Jamaica Rum.
2 Dashes Brown Curacao.
Shake, strain into Goblet with fine ice.
Dress with fruit in season.

LALA ROOK
⅛ Jigger Creme de Vanilla.
⅛ Jigger Jamaica Rum.
⅛ Jigger Brandy.
½ Barspoon Cream.
½ Barspoon Sugar.
Shake, strain and fill glass with Seltzer

LEMON PHOSPHATE
2 Dashes Acid Phosphate.
1 Barspoon Lemon Juice.
1 Pint Lemon Soda.

MAIDEN DREAM
¾ Jigger Benedictine or Cacao.
¼ Jigger Cream Foat.

MAMIE TAYLOR
Use Collin's glass.
1 large lump of Ice.
1 Jigger Scotch Whiskey.
Juice of one-half Lime.
1 Bottle Schweppes Ginger Ale.
Stir well.

MAMIE TAYLOR, SOUTHERN STYLE
Use Long Thin Glass.
Peel of Lemon in one string.
Place in glass so it hangs over.
1 Jigger Scotch Whiskey.
1 Piece Cube Ice.
1 Quart Imported Ginger Ale.

MAMIE TAYLOR'S SISTER
Use Collin's glass.
1 Jigger Dry Gin.
1 Lime squeezed and dropped in.
1 Bottle Imported Ginger Ale.
1 large Cube Ice.

MARTINIQUE
⅓ Jigger Benedictine.
⅓ Jigger Kummel.
⅓ Jigger Cream on top.

MILK AND SELTZER
½ Glass Seltzer.
½ Glass Fresh Milk.
Serve.

MORNING BRACER
⅓ Jigger White Absinthe.
⅔ Jigger Italian Vermouth.
Shake well and strain into Delmonico glass.
Fill with Seltzer.

MORNING BRACER NO. 2
Juice of one-half Orange.
Juice of one-half Lime.
Juice of one-half Lemon.
½ Barspoonful Sugar.
1 Barspoonful Creme de Cacao.
1 White of Egg.
Shake well and strain into a Delmonico glass. Add a little Seltzer.

MORNING STAR
1 Jigger Cream.
½ Jigger Port Wine.
¼ Jigger Scotch.
1 Fresh Egg.
Shake, strain into a long thin glass, fill with Seltzer.

NANA
1 White of Egg.
1 Jigger Brandy.
½ Barspoonful of Powdered Sugar.
Shake, strain into Claret glass.

PARISIAN
1 Jigger Byrrh Wine.
1 Lime Juice.
1 Lump of Ice in glass.
Stir, fill glass with Seltzer and serve.

PARISIAN POUSSE CAFE
⅖ Brown Curacao.
⅖ Kirschwasser.
⅕ Chartreuse.
Use Pousse Cafe Glass.

PEACH BLOW
½ Lemon Juice.
1 Barspoon Sugar.
1 Jigger Gin.
½ Peach.
Shake, strain and fill glass with Seltzer.

PERFECTO
Use Large Glass.
4 Lumps of Ice.
1 Dash Lemon Juice.
1 Lump of Sugar.
2 Slices Pineapple.
Fill glass with champagne.
1 Dash Angostura Bitters.
Dress with fruit in season.

POLLY
Gin Fizz made with Grenadine Syrup instead of using sugar.

PORTO RICO
Gin Rickey made with two dashes of Raspberry Syrup.

PORTER SHANDY
½ Glass of Porter.
½ Glass Light Beer.

PORT STARBOARD
White Curacao.
½ Yellow Chartreuse.
Use Pousse Cafe Glass.

PORT WINE SANGAREE

½ Barspoon Sugar.
1 Jigger Port Wine.
Little Water.
Stir well with spoon.
Grate a little Nutmeg on top and serve.

POUSSE CAFE NO. 1

⅙ Raspberry Syrup
⅙ Maraschino.
⅙ Creme de Menthe Green.
⅙ Curacao Brown.
⅙ Yellow Chartreuse.
⅙ Martell Brandy.
Use Pousse Cafe Glass

POUSSE CAFE NO. 2

⅕ Grenadine Syrup.
⅕ Anisette.
⅕ Creme Yvette.
⅕ Green Chartreuse.
⅕ Martell Brandy.
Use Pousse Cafe Glass.

POUSSE L'AMOUR

⅓ Maraschino.
1 Yolk of Egg.
⅓ Benedictine.
⅓ Brandy.
Sherry Glass.

PROMOTER

½ Lemon Juice.
½ Lime Juice.
1 Barspoonful Sugar.
1 Jigger Sloe Gin.
Fine Ice.
1 Fresh Egg.
Shake well, strain.
Fill glass with Seltzer.

QUEEN CHARLOTTE
¼ Jigger Raspberry Syrup.
1 Jigger French Claret.
1 Lump of Ice.
1 Pint Lemon Soda.
Stir well.
Use Collins glass.

RED SWIZZLE
(Use a Shaker.)
1 Teaspoonful Angostura Bitters.
⅔ Wine-Glass of Whiskey.
⅓ Wine-Glass Water.
Add Syrup or other sweetening to suit taste.
1 Wine-Glass of Shaved Ice.
Shake very well and strain into a fancy Cocktail Glass.

RENAUD'S POUSSE CAFE
⅓ Jigger Maraschino.
⅓ Jigger Curacao.
⅓ Jigger Brandy.
Use Whiskey Glass.

RHINE WINE AND SELTZER
½ Glass Seltzer.
Fill with Rhine Wine and serve.

RUM AND HONEY OR MOLASSES
Use Whiskey Glass into which put 1 Barspoonful of Honey or Molasses.
Let customer help himself with Rum.

SAM WARD
Fill Cocktail Glass with fine Ice.
Remove the Rind from a slice of Lemon and fit it inside of the Rim of the Cocktail Glass, then fill with yellow Chartreuse or any cordial the customer may prefer, and serve.

SHANDY GAFF

Half a Glass of Ale.
Half a Glass of Ginger Ale.

SHERRY AND BITTERS

1 Dash of Bitters and fill Glass with
Sherry Wine and serve.

SHERRY AND EGG

1 Barspoonful of Sherry Wine.
1 Fresh Egg and fill Glass with Sherry
until it floats and serve.

SHERRY CHICKEN

Sherry Egg Nogg.

SHERRY WINE SANGAREE

Prepare this drink same as Port Wine
Sangaree, substituting Sherry for Port.

SILVER DREAM

Juice of ½ Lemon.
½ Barspoonful Sugar.
1 White of egg.
1 Jigger Dry Gin.
Shake well, strain into Claret Glass,
then squirt a little Seltzer on top and
serve.

SINGLE STANDARD

Bourbon Whiskey Rickey in Lemonade
Glass.

SNOWBALL

1 White of Egg.
1 Barspoon Sugar.
1 Jigger Rum or Brandy.
Shake, strain and fill Glass with Imported Ginger Ale and serve.
Use Collins Glass.

SODA NEGUS PUNCH BOWL

4 dashes Angostura Bitters.
1 Pint of Port Wine.
10 or 12 Lumps of Loaf Sugar.
12 Whole Cloves.
1 Teaspoon Nutmeg.
Put above ingredients into Saucepan,
warm and stir well. Do not let it boil.
Remove this mixture to cool, then add
1 Pint Soda in Punch and serve in
Cups.

SOOTHER

½ Lemon Juice.
1 Barspoon Sugar.
¼ Jigger Brandy.
¼ Jigger Apple Jack.
¼ Jigger Curacao.
Shake, strain into Goblet filled with fine
ice.

SOUL KISS

½ Barspoon Sugar.
1 Orange Juice.
½ Jigger Byrrh Wine.
¼ Jigger Rye.
¼ Jigger French Vermouth.
Shake, strain into Lemonade Glass and
fill with Seltzer.

SOUL KISS NO. 2

½ Jigger Maraschino.
½ Jigger Creme Yvette.
1 Maraschino Cherry.

SPECIAL

1 Jigger Orange Juice.
1 Jigger Lemon Juice.
1 Jigger Dry Gin.
1 Barspoon Sugar.
Shake well and pour ice and all into
Goblet and serve.

ST. CROIX RUM CRUSTA

3 Dashes of Syrup.
1 Dash Angostura Bitters.
1 Dash Orange Bitters.
1 Jigger St. Croix Rum.
2 or 3 dashes Maraschino.
Mix well and strain into long Glass and put the peel from one lemon in one string into Glass after dipping in Powdered Sugar.
Little Seltzer on Top.

STINGER

½ Jigger Brandy.
½ Jigger Creme de Menthe White.
1 Lemon Peel.
Shake, strain into Cocktail Glass.

STONE FENCE

1 Jigger Rye Whiskey
2 Lumps Ice.
Fill Glass with Cider.
Stir well and serve.

STONEWALL

1 Barspoon Sugar.
2 Lumps of Ice.
1 Jigger Whiskey.
1 Pint of Schweppes Club Soda.
Stir up well with spoon and serve.

SUSIE TAYLOR

½ Lime Juice.
1 Jigger Jamaica Rum.
1 Pint Imported Ginger Ale.

SUISSESS

¾ Jigger White Absinthe.
¼ Jigger Anisette.
1 White of Egg.
Shake well in Shaker, strain in Delmonico Glass.

SUISETTE

½ Lemon Juice.
2 Dashes Absinthe.
1 Barspoon of Sugar.
⅓ Jigger Italian Vermouth.
⅔ Jigger Brandy.
Shake, strain into long Glass, fill wit'
Seltzer.

TEA SHAKE

1 Jigger of Tea.
1 Whole Fresh Egg.
½ Barspoon Sugar.
Shake well and strain into Claret Glass
and serve.

THREE-QUARTER

⅓ Jigger Yellow Chartreuse.
⅓ Jigger Curacao.
⅓ Jigger Brandy.

TIT FLOAT

Curacao with little Whip Cream on top
and place a small piece Red Cherry in
the center and serve.

TIP-TOP BRACER

Take Highball Glass into which put 1
small lump of Ice.
1 Split Sparkling Water.
2 Dashes Celery Bitters.
A little Salt and stir well with spoon
and serve.

TOBIE TOBIAS

½ Jigger Brandy.
½ Jigger Apricot Brandy.
Lemon Peel, shake, strain into Cocktail Glass.

TOM AND JERRY

Use large bowl.
Take the whites of any number of Eggs and beat to a stiff froth.
Add 1½ Barspoons of Sugar to each Egg.
Beat the yolks of the eggs separate.
Stir well together and beat till you have a stiff batter. Add to this as much bicarbonate of Soda as will cover a nickel. Stir up frequently, so that eggs will not separate or settle.
To serve:
Put 1 tablespoon full of batter into Tom and Jerry Mug.
1 Jigger Rum and Brandy mixed.
Fill up with boiling water or milk, grate nutmeg on top, stir with spoon and serve.

TWENTIETH CENTURY

Juice of ½ Lime.
Juice of ½ Lemon.
1 Barspoon Sugar.
1 Jigger Bourbon.
1 Dash Jamaica Rum.
Shake well and strain into Highball Glass. Fill with Ginger Ale or Seltzer.

VELVET

1 Pint Paul Garrett Champagne.
1 Pint Stout.

VICHY

Do not mix in White or Red Wines, as it turns black.
It blends well with Scotch and Irish Whiskey.

WHITE CAP

Benedictine with Cream on Top.

WHITE HORSE

1 Lump of Ice.
Juice of ½ Orange.
2 Dashes Angostura Bitters.
1 Jigger Scotch Whiskey.
1 Pint Imported Ginger Ale.
Use Collins' Glass.

WHITE PLUSH

½ Jigger Rye
¼ Jigger Maraschino.
1 Egg.
1 Small Bottle Milk.
Shake, strain into thin Glass and serve.

WIDOW'S DREAM

⅔ Jigger Benedictine.
1 Egg.
1 Jigger Cream.
Shake, strain and serve.

WIDOW'S KISS

¼ Jigger Parfait Amour.
¼ Jigger Yellow Chartreuse.
¼ Jigger Benedcitine.
Beaten White of Egg on Top.

WINDOW'S KISS NO. 2

1 Yolk of Egg.
1 Barspoonful Sugar.
1 Jigger Rye Whiskey.
Shake well, then fill High Ball Glass
½ full with Seltzer and float above mixture on top.

WHISKEY FLOAT

Fill Glass ½ full of Fizz Water, pour
1 Jigger Bourbon or Rye Whiskey slowly
on top of Fizz Water and serve.

WHISKEY FIX

1 Barspoonful Sugar.
Juice of ½ Lemon.
1 Jigger Whiskey.
Shake and strain into Goblet and dress
with Fruit in season.

PUNCHES

AMERICAN BEAUTY PUNCH

1 Barspoonful Creme de Menthe in Goblet filled with fine Ice.
Mix Juice of ½ Orange.
½ Barspoonful Sugar.
½ Jigger Brandy.
½ Jigger French Vermouth in Mixing Glass.
Shake, strain into Goblet.
Dress with Fruit and Mint.
Top off with 1 Barspoonful of Port Wine.

A LA ROMAINE PUNCH

1 Quart Rum.
2 Barspoonfuls Angostura Bitters.
Juice of 10 Lemons.
Juice of 3 Oranges.
2 Pounds Granulated Sugar.
10 Fresh Eggs.
Dissolve the Sugar in the Lemon Juice and Orange Juice.
Add the Rind of 1 Orange, strain through a Seive into Bowl and add the Whites of Eggs beaten to a froth.
Place the Bowl on Ice until cold, then stir until thoroughly mixed.
Serve in Delmonico Glass.

ASTOR PUNCH

½ Jigger White Creme de Menthe.
Fine Ice in Goblet.
½ Jigger Sloe Gin on top.
Dress with Fruit in season.

BILL MEYER PUNCH

1 Dash Lemon Juice.
1 Lump of Loaf Sugar.
2 Slices Pineapple.
2 Slices Orange.

(Continued)

BILL MEYER PUNCH—Cont'd.

1 Slice Lemon.
Use large Glass, with 5 Lumps of clear Ice.
Fill up with Pommery Champagne.
Stir well.
Dress with Cherries and serve.

BISHOP PUNCH—(Pitcher)

½ Lemon Juice.
1 Jigger Syrup.
1 Jigger Jamaica Rum.
1 Pint Claret (for Party of 2 or 3).
Dress with Fruit and Mint.

BRANDY MILK PUNCH

1 Jigger Brandy.
1 Dash Jamaica Rum.
1 Barspoonful Sugar.
Milk.
Shake, strain and put little Nutmeg on top.

BRANDY PUNCH

Use Goblet.
Crushed Ice.
1 Jigger Brandy.
1 Dash Sugar.
2 Dashes Raspberry Syrup.
1 Dash Maraschino.
Dress with Mint.
Stir well.
Seltzer.

BORDELAISE PUNCH

Juice of one-half Lemon.
2 Dashes Raspberry Syrup.
1 Barspoon Sugar.
1 Jigger Kirschwasser in Goblet with Fine Ice.
2 Slices Lime.
2 Slices Lemon.
Stir well and squirt a little Seltzer on top.

BOSTON MILK PUNCH

½ Jigger Bourbon Whiskey.
½ Jigger St. Croix Rum.
1 Small Barspoonful Sugar.
½ Bottle Milk.
Shake, strain.

BOURBON OR RYE WHISKEY PUNCH

Juice of ½ Lemon.
1 Small Barspoonful Sugar.
1 Jigger Bourbon or Rye.
Shake, strain into Goblet with fine Ice.
Dress with Fruit and serve.

BRUNSWICK PUNCH

Milk Shake made without Sugar.
Use Raspberry Syrup instead and
½ Pony Curacao.

BULL MOOSE PUNCH

⅓ Jigger Rye Whiskey.
⅓ Jigger Bourbon Whiskey.
⅓ Jigger Dry Gin.
1 Dash Angostura Bitters.
1 Dash Orange Bitters.
3 Dashes Syrup.
Shake, strain into Goblet.
Fill with crushed Ice and dress with
Fruit.

CARDINAL PUNCH

Cover the bottom of a Punch Bowl with
Loaf Sugar in 2 Quarts Sparkling Water,
2 Quarts Claret, 1 Pint Cognac, 1 Pint
Rum.
1 Pint Sparkling Moselle.
1 Jigger Vermouth.
3 Oranges, sliced.
1 Lemon, sliced.
¼ Pineapple, sliced.
1 Large Piece of Ice, and serve in Punch
Glasses.

CHAMPAGNE PUNCH
1 Gallon Punch Bowl.
Juice of 4 Lemons.
1 Pony Maraschino Holland.
3 Ponies Martell Brandy.
1 Pony Brown Curacao.
1 Dash Yellow Chartreuse.
2 Quarts Pommery Champagne.
2 Quarts Apollinaris or any other brand
the Customer desires.
Sugar to taste. Fruits.

CHAMPAGNE PUNCH NO. 2
1 Gallon Punch Bowl.
2 Quarts Pommery Champagne.
1 Quart Rhine Wine.
1 Quart Apollinaris.
1 Quart Lemon Juice.
2 Jiggers Curacao.
1 Jigger Apple Jack.
1 Jigger Brandy.
Sugar to taste.
Dress with Fruit.

CLARET PUNCH
Goblet fine Ice.
1 Jigger Barton & Guestier Claret.
4 Dashes Lemon Juice.
2 Dashes Curacao.
2 Dashes Syrup.
Dress with Fruits.

CLARET PUNCH
1 Gallon.
Juice of 6 Lemons.
2 Ponies Curacao.
4 Ponies Brandy.
2 Dashes Benedictine.
2 Quarts of Claret.
2 Quarts of Apollinaris.
Sugar to taste.
Punch Bowl. Fruits.

COMBINATION PUNCH

Juice of ½ Lemon.
Juice of ½ Lime.
Juice of ½ Orange.
1 Jigger Rye or Bourbon Whiskey.
Shake, strain into Goblet filled with
crushed Ice and dress with Fruit.

CREAM PUNCH

1 Barspoonful of Granulated Sugar.
½ Jigger Brandy.
½ Jigger Maraschino.
1 Small Bottle Cream.
1 Dash Curacao.
Shake, strain into Punch Glass.

CREOLE PUNCH

1 Jigger French Claret.
½ Jigger Brandy.
2 Dashes Hungarian Apricot Brandy.
2 Dashes Jamaica Rum.
1 Barspoonful Syrup.
Crushed Ice into Goblet.
Dress with Fruit.
When served Hot add Spices and Lemon
Peel and serve in Silver Pitcher.

CURACAO PUNCH

¼ of 1 Lemon Juice.
Sugar to taste.
¾ Jigger Curacao.
¼ Jigger Brandy.
Shake, strain into Goblet of fine Ice.
Dress with Fruit.

ELMWOOD PUNCH

4 Pints Grape Juice.
1 Pint Claret.
1 Pint Pommery Champagne.
2 Spoons Grated Pineapple.
Sugar to taste.
Dress with Fruit in season.

EMPRESS PUNCH

2 Crushed Lumps Sugar.
3 Dashes Angostura Bitters.
4 or 5 Lumps of Ice.
1 Split Champagne.
Dress with Fruit and put little Mint on top and add 2 thin Slices of Limes and serve.

FISH HOUSE PUNCH

One Only.
Juice of one-half Lemon.
⅔ Jigger Rum.
⅛ Jigger Brandy.
1 Dash Peach Brandy.
½ Barspoonful Sugar.
Shake, strain into Water Goblet filled with fine Ice.
Dress with Fruit.

FISH HOUSE PUNCH

In the original receipt for the Fish House Punch, Cider was used in place of Champagne, and no Water used.
Juice of 4 Dozen Lemons.
1½ Pounds Granulated Sugar.
1 Pint Curacao.
1 Pint Jamaica Rum.
1 Pint Benedictine.
1 Quart Peach Brandy.
4 Quarts Green River Whiskey.
Put above Ingredients in a Jug (not sealed) for about 10 days. Shake occasionally. Strain through cheesecloth and serve in Punch Bowl.
Add 1 Quart Champagne.
1 Quart of Sparkling Water to about 3 Quarts of the Punch.

GOODMAN PUNCH

½ Lime Juice.
¼ Jigger Sherry.

(Continued)

Historic Cookbooks of the World

GOODMAN PUNCH—Cont'd

¾ Jigger Rye Whiskey.
½ Barspoon Granulated Sugar.
Shake, strain into Goblet.
Dress with Fruit.

HARDING PUNCH

2 Gallons.
1 Quart St. Croix Rum.
1 Quart Brandy.
1 Quart Pommery Champagne.
⅔ Quart Arrack.
1 Quart Peach Brandy.
3 Pounds Granulated Sugar.
⅛ Pound Green Tea, Steeped.
2 Quarts Ice Water.

HERALD PUNCH

2 Jiggers Orange Juice.
1 Jigger Rye Whiskey.
Goblet, fine Ice, dress with Fruit and
Dash of Rum on top.

HOLLAND GIN PUNCH

Juice of ½ Lime.
1 Small Barspoonful Sugar.
1 Jigger Holland Gin.
Goblet, with fine Ice.
Shake and strain.
Dress with Fruit.
Tom, Sloe, Dry Gin Punch are the same
as Holland Gin Punch.

HOT CLARET PUNCH

Juice of one-half Lemon.
1 Barspoonful of Sugar.
Cinnamon to taste.
1 Jigger Claret.
Lemon Peel.
Boil this and strain into Glass Cup and
serve.

IRISH WHISKEY PUNCH

Juice of ½ Lemon.
1 Barspoonful Sugar.
1 Jigger Irish Whiskey.
Shake and strain into Goblet with fine
Ice. Dress with Fruits in season.

KNICKERBOCKER PUNCH

½ Lime Juice.
1 Barspoonful Sugar.
1 Jigger St. Croix Rum.
Shake, strain into Goblet with fine Ice.
Dress with Fruit and put 1 Dash Claret
on top.

LORD BALTIMORE PUNCH

Juice of 2 Limes.
1 Barspoonful Sugar.
1 Jigger McCallum's Perfection Scotch
Whiskey.
2 Dashes Benedictine.
Shake, strain into Goblet.
Dress with Fruit.

MERRY WIDOW PUNCH

Juice of ½ Lemon.
½ Barspoon Sugar.
1 Jigger Sloe Gin.
1 Dash Vanilla.
Shake, strain into Goblet with fine Ice
and float 1 Barspoonful Cream on top.

MILK PUNCH

1 Barspoonful Sugar.
⅔ Jigger Green River Whiskey.
⅓ Jigger French Brandy.
1 Dash Rum.
Fill Mixing Glass with Fresh, Rich Milk.
Shake well. Strain in Lemonade Glass
and serve little Nutmeg on top.

MILLIONAIRE PUNCH

Juice of 1 Lemon.
1 Dash of Lime Juice.
1 Barspoonful Sugar.
1 Jigger of very best Whiskey.
2 Dashes of Grenadine Syrup.
Shake well.
Strain into Goblet and decorate with Fruit.
1 Dash Creme de Menthe on top.

MONTICELLO PUNCH

1 Pint Pommery Sec Champagne.
1 Jigger Brandy.
½ Lemon Juice.
Sugar to taste.
Dress with Fruits in season.

PEACH BRANDY PUNCH

Juice ½ Lemon.
1 Barspoonful Sugar.
1 Jigger Peach Brandy.
Shake, strain into Goblet filled with fine Ice. Dress with Fruit.

PONY PUNCH

Juice of 6 Lemons.
Juice of ½ Pineapple.
1 Quart Bourbon Whiskey.
1 Quart Green Tea.
½ Pint Jamaica Rum.
½ Pint Maraschino, French.
Mix well together and serve in Punch Glass. Dress with Fruits.

REGENT PUNCH

1 Lemon, sliced.
1 Orange, sliced.
1 Can Pineapple and Juice.
¼ Pint St. Croix Rum.
½ Pint Rye Whiskey.

(Continued)

REGENT PUNCH—Cont'd.

18 Lumps of Sugar.
Mix in Punch Bowl and let stand 2
hours in cold place; then add quickly
1 Pint of Tea and mix slowly with above.
When ready to serve set on table and add
1 Quart of Paul Garrett Champagne.

RHINE WINE PUNCH

1 Gallon.
Juice of 8 Lemons.
2 Ponies of Brandy.
2 Ponies of Curacao.
1 Pony of Benedictine.
2 Quarts Rhine Wine.
2 Quarts Sparkling Water.
Sugar to taste.

ROMAN PUNCH

Juice of ½ Lemon.
½ Pony Water.
1 Barspoonful Granulated Sugar.
¼ Jigger Rum.
¼ Jigger Brown Curacao.
½ Jigger Brandy.
Shake well, strain into Goblet.
Dress with Fruit in season and add
little Port Wine on top.

ROOSEVELT PUNCH

Moddle ½ Lemon.
1 Barspoonful Sugar.
1 Jigger Apple Brandy.
½ Pony Water.
Shake, strain into Goblet.
Dress with Fruit and little Brandy on top.

RUM PUNCH

Juice of ½ Lemon or Lime.
1 Barspoonful Sugar.
1 Jigger Rum.
1 Dash Brandy.
Shake, strain into Goblet and dress with
Fruit.

SALOME PUNCH

1 Barspoonful Sugar.
1 Egg.
1 Pony Curacao.
1 Pint Milk.
Shake and strain into Goblets. Serve.

SAUTERNES PUNCH

1 Gallon.
Juice of 4-6 Lemons.
2 Jiggers Brandy.
1 Jigger Apple Brandy.
1 Jigger Pineapple Juice.
2 Dashes Yellow Chartreuse.
2 Quarts B. & G. Sauternes.
2 Quarts Apollinaris.
Sugar to taste.
Dress with Fruits.

SCHLEY PUNCH

Juice and Rind of 1 Lime.
1 Barspoonful of Sugar.
⅓ Jigger St. Croix Rum.
⅔ Jigger Bourbon or Rye Whiskey.
Shake, strain into Goblet with fine Ice.
Dress with Fruit and put little Mint on
top.

SCOTCH WHISKEY PUNCH

Juice of ½ Lemon.
1 Barspoonful of Sugar.
1 Jigger Scotch Whiskey.
Shake and strain into Goblet.
Dress with Fruit.

SHERIDAN PUNCH

Plain Lemonade, with ½ Jigger Rye Whiskey, float.

SHERRY CHICKEN PUNCH

1 Barspoonful Sugar.
1 Jigger Sherry.
1 Egg.
3 Jiggers of Milk.
1 Dash of Brandy.
Shake, strain into thin Glass and serve.

SOOTHER PUNCH

Juice of ½ Lemon.
1 Barspoonful Sugar.
¼ Jigger Brandy.
¼ Jigger Jamaica Rum.
¼ Jigger Apple Jack.
¼ Jigger Curacao.
Shake, strain into Goblet with fine Ice.
Dress with Fruit.

SPECIAL PUNCH

1 Jigger Orange Juice.
1 Jigger Lemon Juice.
1 Jigger Dry Gin.
½ Plain Syrup.
Shake and strain into Goblet with only Ice in that and serve.

STEINWAY PUNCH

Juice of 1 Lemon.
1 Barspoonful Sugar.
¾ Jigger Rye Whiskey.
¼ Jigger Curacao.
Shake and strain into Punch Glass.
Fill with Seltzer.

WALDORF PUNCH

Juice of ½ Lemon.
1 Barspoonful Sugar.
1 Jigger Rye Whiskey.
½ Pony Water.
Shake, strain into Goblet with crushed
Ice. Dress with Fruit and float little
Claret on top.

WHISKEY PUNCH—(Old Fashion)

1 Quart.
1 Quart Bourbon Whiskey.
3 Jiggers of Lemon Juice.
2 Jiggers of Curacao.
½ Pint Plain Water or Sparkling.
1 Jigger Plain Syrup.
1 Long Cube Ice.
3 or 4 Slices of Cucumber Rind.
Decorate with Fruit and Mint.

———

No mixed drink is perfect unless ingredients used
are perfect.

PUNCHES—Non Alcoholic

ARCTIC PUNCH

1 Jigger Raspberry Syrup.
Juice of 2 Limes.
2 Pints Schweppes Ginger Ale.
1 Pint Cold English Tea in Pitcher.
Dress with Fruits and Mint.

BLACKSTONE NECTAR

Juice of 1 small Orange.
Juice of 1 small Lemon.
Raspberry Syrup to taste.
Shake, strain into Goblet with Crushed
Ice. Fill Glass with Seltzer, dress with
Fruit and 3 or 4 sprigs of Mint on top.

CONCLAVE PUNCH

Juice of 1 Orange.
1 Jigger Raspberry Syrup.
1 Barspoonful Sugar.
3 Jiggers Fresh Milk.
Shake, strain into thin Glass and serve.

CUBAN MILK PUNCH

1 Jigger Vanilla.
1 Egg.
1 Barspoonful Sugar.
3 Jiggers Fresh Milk.
Shake, strain and serve in thin Glass.

GINGER ALE PUNCH

Juice of ½ Orange.
Juice of ½ Lemon.
Grenadine Syrup to taste.
Shake, strain into Goblet filled with
crushed Ice.
Add 1 Split of Ginger Ale.
Dress with Fruit and serve 2 or 3 Sprigs
of Mint on top.

MINT PUNCH

1 Bunch Fresh Mint moddled in long, thin Glass.
1 Cube of Ice.
1 Pint Imported Ginger Ale.

WALDORF PUNCH

Juice of 1 Orange.
Juice of 1 Lemon.
1 Fresh Egg.
Shake, strain.
Fill Glass with Seltzer.

MILK SHAKE

½ Barspoonful Sugar.
1 Pint Fresh Milk.
1 Dash Raspberry Syrup.
Shake well.

RICKEYS

GIN RICKEY

Juice of Half a Lime.
1 Lump of Cut Ice.
Then allow the Customer to help himself
to Gin and fill Glass with Seltzer.
Stir with spoon.

IRISH WHISKEY RICKEY
BOURBON OR RYE RICKEY
SCOTCH RICKEY
RUM RICKEY
BRANDY RICKEY
APRICOT BRANDY RICKEY

Make these same as Gin Rickey, using
either Whiskey or Cognac instead of
Gin.

GIN BUCK

Same as Gin Rickey, except use Ginger
Ale instead of Seltzer.

No mixed drink is perfect unless ingredients use
are perfect.

SOURS

AMER PICON SOUR
Juice of ½ Lemon.
Juice of ½ Lime.
1 Small Barspoonful of Sugar.
¼ Jigger Grenadine Syrup.
¾ Jigger Amer Picon.
Shake well and strain into Sour Glass,
then put in 1 Slice of Orange, 1 Slice of
Pineapple and 1 Cherry.

BRANDY SOUR
Juice of ½ Lemon.
1 Barspoonful of Granulated Sugar.
1 Jigger Martell Brandy.
Shake and strain.
Dress with Fruit.

BRUNSWICK SOUR
Juice of 1 Small Lemon.
1 Barspoonful of Granulated Sugar.
1 Jigger Rye Whiskey.
Shake well and strain and float Claret on
top.
Same Fruits as Amer Picon Sour.

CANADIAN WHISKEY SOUR
Juice of ½ Lemon.
Juice of ½ Lime.
1 Barspoonful Sugar.
1 Jigger Canadian Whiskey.
1 Dash of Grenadine.
Shake well.
Dress with Fruit.

CHAMPAGNE SOUR
Juice of ½ fresh Lemon.
1 Lump of Sugar, dissolved.
Fill with Champagne.
Stir well.
Dress with Fruit in season.

DOUBLE STANDARD SOUR

Juice of 1 Lime.
½ Barspoonful Sugar.
½ Jigger Rye Whiskey.
½ Jigger Dry Gin.
2 Dashes Raspberry Syrup.
Shake, strain.
1 Squirt Seltzer on top.

EGG SOUR

1 Barspoonful of Sugar.
Juice of ½ Lemon.
Yolk of 1 Egg.
1 Dash Anisette.
1 Jigger Brandy.
Shake well.

GIN SOUR

Juice of 1 Small Lemon.
1 Barspoonful Granulated Sugar.
1 Jigger Dry Gin, or Tom, Holland, or
High and Dry, or Sloe Gin, or whatever
brand the Customer desires.
Shake and strain into Sour Glass.
Dress with Fruit.

GRENADINE SOUR

Juice of 1 Small Lemon.
⅓ Jigger Grenadine Syrup.
1 Jigger Bourbon Whiskey.
Shake well and strain into Sour Glass.
Dress with Fruit.

GRENADINE GIN SOUR

Juice of ½ Lemon.
⅓ Jigger Grenadine.
1 Jigger Dry Gin.
Shake well, strain into Sour Glass and
Dress with Fruit.

HANCOCK SOUR

Juice of 1 Lime.
1 Barspoonful Sugar.
1 Jigger Bourbon Whiskey.
1 Dash of Rum.
Shake and strain.
Dress with Fruit.
1 Squirt Seltzer on top.

IRISH WHISKEY SOUR

Same as Whiskey Sour, except use Irish
Whiskey in place of Rye or Bourbon.

JAMAICA RUM SOUR

Juice of 1 Lemon.
1 Barspoonful of Sugar.
1 Jigger Jamaica Rum.
1 Dash Curacao.
Shake, strain.
Dress with Fruit.

JERSEY SOUR

Juice of 1 Lemon.
1 Barspoonful of Sugar.
1 Jigger Apple Jack.
Shake, strain.
Sqeeze Lemon Peel on Top.
Dress with Fruit.

MILLIONAIRE SOUR

Juice of 1 Lime.
1 Dash Lemon Juice.
⅓ Jigger of Grenadine.
⅔ Jigger of Rye Whiskey.
3 or 4 Dashes of Curacao.
Shake well.
Dress with Fruit.

ROOSEVELT SOUR

½ Lemon Juice.
1 Dash Lime Juice.
1 Jigger Apple Jack.
1 Barspoonful of Sugar.
Shake well.
Dress with Fruit in season.

RUM SOUR

½ Lemon Juice.
1 Barspoonful of Sugar.
1 Jigger of Rum, whichever is preferred
by your Customer.
Shake well and strain into Sour Glass.
Dress with Fruit.

SARATOGA SOUR

Juice of ½ Lemon.
Barspoonful of Sugar.
1 Jigger Rye Whiskey.
Shake well.
Dress with Fruit.
Squirt Seltzer, and float Claret on top.

SCOTCH SOUR

Same as Rum Sour, except use McCallum
Perfection Scotch Whiskey in place of
Rum.

SILVER SOUR

Juice of 1 Lemon.
1 Barspoonful of Sugar.
¼ Jigger Jamaica Rum.
¼ Jigger Brandy.
¼ Jigger Curacao.
¼ Jigger Apple Jack.
Shake well, strain into Sour Glass.
Dress with Fruit.

SOUTHERN SOUR

Juice of ½ Lemon.
1 Barspoonful of Sugar.
1 Jigger St. Croix Rum.
Shake and strain.
Dress with Fruit and float Claret on top.

TOURAINE SOUR

Whiskey Sour, with Dash of Benedictine.
Float Claret on top.

WHISKEY SOUR

Juice of ½ Lemon.
1 Barspoonful of Granulated Sugar.
1 Jigger Bourbon or Rye.
Shake and strain into Sour Glass.
Dress with Fruit.

SLINGS

BRANDY SLING

1 Crushed Lump of Sugar in Old Fashion Glass.
1 Jigger Brandy.
1 Lump Ice.

GIN SLING

1 Crushed Lump Sugar in Old Fashion Glass.
1 Jigger Gin.
1 Lemon Peel.
1 Lump Ice.
Stir.

IRISH SLING

In Old Fashion Glass.
Crush 1 Lump Sugar.
Add 1 Jigger Irish Whiskey.
2 Small Lumps of Ice.

RUM SLING

1 Crushed Lump of Sugar in Old Fashion Glass.
1 Jigger Jamaica Rum.
1 Lump of Ice.

SCOTCH SLING

1 Crushed Lump of Sugar in Old Fashion Glass.
1 Jigger Scotch.
1 Orange Peel.
1 Lump of Sugar.

WHISKEY SLING

In Old Fashion Glass.
Crush 1 Lump of Sugar.
Add 1 Jigger Bourbon.

SMASH

BRANDY SMASH
In Old Fashion Glass.
Crush ½ Lump of Sugar with 3 Sprigs
of Mint.
1 Jigger Brandy.
1 Lump of Ice.
Stir and serve.

GIN SMASH
Same as Brandy Smash.
Substitute Gin for Brandy.

MINT SMASH
Crush some Mint and ½ Lump Sugar in
Old Fashion Glass.
1 Jigger Whiskey.
1 Lump Ice.
Stir and serve.

WHISKEY SMASH
Same as Mint Smash.

No mixed drink is perfect unless ingredients used
are perfect.

TODDIES

APPLE TODDY

Crush ½ Lump of Sugar with little
Water in an Old Fashion Glass.
1 Lump of Ice.
1 Jigger Apple Jack.
1 Lemon Peel.
Stir.

BRANDY TODDY

Same as Apple Toddy.
Use Brandy instead of Apple Jack.

GIN TODDY

Same as Brandy Toddy.
Use Gin instead of Brandy.

KENTUCKY TODDY

Crush ½ Lump of Sugar with a little
Water in an Old Fashion Glass.
1 Jigger Green River Bourbon.
1 Lump Ice.
Stir.

MINT TODDY

Crush ½ Lump of Sugar and 3 Sprigs of
Mint in Old Fashion Glass.
1 Jigger Bourbon.
1 Lump of Ice.
Stir.

PEACH TODDY

Crush ½ Lump of Sugar in Old Fashion
Glass.
1 Jigger Peach Brandy.
1 Lump Ice.
1 Lemon Peel.

PENDENNIS TODDY

Crush ½ Lump of Sugar with a little
Water in an Old Fashion Glass.
1 Jigger Bourbon.
1 Lump of Ice.

RUM TODDY

Same as Peach Toddy.
Use 1 Jigger Jamaica Rum instead of
Peach Brandy.

SCOTCH TODDY

Same as Rum Toddy.
Use Scotch Whiskey instead of Rum.

SOUTHERN TODDY

½ Lump of Sugar crushed in Old Fashion Glass.
1 Jigger Bourbon.
1 Lemon Peel.
Stir.

WHISKEY TODDY

Crush ½ Lump of Sugar with a little
Water in Old Fashion Glass.
1 Jigger Bourbon.
1 Lemon Peel.
Stir.

Etiquette of the Glass

THE careful selection of the proper glass to use in serving a beverage is of no small importance. Good judgment and refined taste in observing the rules of etiquette in this respect on all occasions add a finishing touch to the enjoyment of the drink. The best authorities nearly all agree on certain shapes or styles of glasses and differ only in matter of ornament or size, or a slight variation in form. The host or hostess is safe in being guided by the patterns prescribed in this book as the latest and most popular in use.

Pony Brandy

Whiskey

Pousse Cafe

Cut Cordial

Absinthe Drip

Cordial

Claret

Sherry

Water Goblet

Tom Collins

Fancy Fizz

Brandy & Soda

Pilsener

Cocktail, New Shape

Horses Neck

Creme de Menthe

Ale

Milk Punch

Toddy

Rhine Wine

Rhine Wine

Moselle Wine

Champagne

Delmonico
Champagne Tumbler

Saucer Champagne

Hollowstem
Champagne

Classic Cocktail Guides and Retro Bartender Books

Therapeutic Values of Wines

CENTURIES of experience have confirmed that wine is a marvelous product for man either in health or illness, if he makes judicious use of it, according to his constitution.

High medical authorities and scientists throughout the world acknowledge that wine spirits and malt liquors used as a beverage are very beneficial to health when taken in moderation and are absolutely necessary in many cases of fever, nervous exhaustion, debility and convalescence.

Old people are greatly benefited by daily drinking of good wines in moderate quantity. A poet once said "that the man who drinks wine must necessarily have more exalted thoughts than he who drinks water."

Wine invigorates the mind and body, and gives life an additional charm, but temperance and moderation are virtues essential to our happiness.

The good effect of wines as a food is due to their stimulating operation on the nervous system and muscular lining of the stomach, by which the same is excited to greater action and produces a healthy flow of the gastric juices.

Wine being the pure juice of the grape properly fermented and aged is without question a healthful beverage to take with meals, and if those who drink ice water would use wine instead, they would find their digestion better and their general health improved.

The Standard for Champagne Quality

Pommery

"SEC" AND "BRUT"

**THE HIGHEST
ATTAINMENT
IN THE ART OF
WINE MAKING**

═══

Delicious Flavor,
Rich, Fragrant
Bouquet

═══

UNSURPASSED
BRILLIANCY

From the

Celebrated Wine Cellars

of

POMMERY & GRENO

RHEIMS
FRANCE

HOW TO OBTAIN BEST RESULTS

In getting up the collection of recipes which appear in this little booklet, it has been my aim to satisfy the palate of the most critical connoisseur.

However, it should be understood, that no matter where these drinks may be made, at the club, cafe or your private house, it is only by using the best quality of goods that proper and satisfactory results can be obtained.

Sugar, bitters, fruit juices, etc., are great agents of assistance in producing a palatable drink even out of inferior whiskies, gins and brandies.

However, the man who cares for the welfare of his patrons, and wishes his goods to have the proper after effects, will use quality and honest materials at all times.

HOW TO HANDLE AND SERVE WINES

Having made wine culture and distillation a lifetime study and profession, with experience in different countries, the writer takes pleasure in saying a few words regarding the proper handling, conditioning and serving of wines, also as to their therapeutic properties.

Beginning with Champagne, I may say that the quality of this wine very often suffers greatly by being placed into the hands of inexperienced people.

Upon receipt of a shipment of champagne or any other sparkling wine, the same should be promptly unpacked and every bottle inspected as to the soundness of the cork. All such that show signs of leakage should be be used first, while the others should be stored lying down and be given a rest for several days.

THE KING OF WINES
THE WINE OF KINGS

F. Chauvenet

NUITS FRANCE

Sparkling
Red
Burgundy

The choicest vintages from the
Celebrated Cote d'Or Region, France

RICH, BRILLIANT COLOR
AND FRAGRANT BOUQUET

POSITIVELY THE FINEST OF ALL
RED, SPARKLING WINES

No Wine List is complete without it

When conditioning Champagne for service, the chilling of the same should be slowly and carefully done by placing the warm bottle in a refrigerator for several hours and not packed in ice until shortly before serving.

Taking wines from the case or shelf and packing them in ice is a very serious mistake, as chilling too quickly robs them of their life and vinosity.

Should the time for conditioning be short, place the wine in a bucket of cold water as it runs from the faucet, adding a few lumps of ice every ten to fifteen minutes and in this way preserve the good quality of your wine.

Old vintage wines should be served at a temperature of about 45 degrees while the young vintages showing more life are served best at about 38 degrees.

Non-vintage Champagnes may be served at a temperature of 32 degrees.

Upon taking the bottle from the cooler it should be well wrapped with a napkin so the warm hand of the waiter will not come in contact with the bottle and agitate the wine.

Cap, wire and string should be carefully removed, head of bottle cleaned and the cork slowly drawn so all gas may be retained in the wine.

Care should be taken to have the glasses clean and dry and to always serve the host first. This is an old time custom which is done to give the host a chance to taste the wine before serving his guests.

Glasses should not be filled more than within one-fourth inch from the brim.

The Ritz champagne glass is unquestionably the best and most practical in the serving of sparkling wines because it is compact and does not agitate

Famous Vintage Wines From France's Greatest Vineyards

BARTON & GUESTIER
Clarets and Sauternes
BORDEAUX, FRANCE

The Choicest Chateau Bottlings

Served in the World's Most
Exclusive Clubs and Hotels

House Established
in 1725

the wine, as is the case with a hollow stem glass.

The saucer glass being wide and shallow, should never be used, as it gives the wine too much surface, causing the wine to quickly become warm and losing its effervescence.

The proper time for serving Champagne is with the last meat course of the dinner. Being served cold, the carbonic gas becomes "caged" and drinking the same between two warm courses, the gas becomes released, causing one to belch and bring small particles of food into the throat and render the stomach sour.

Having enjoyed a meal of several courses, the gastric juices are not strong enough to properly take care of same and fermentation, creating a gas, sets in before digestion is complete.

It is at this time that Champagne will do the work it is intended for and at once relieve you of that oppressive and uncomfortable feeling.

In case of illness, especially typhoid fever, where the stomach has become dormant from not being supplied with solid food for a long time, Champagne should be the first wine given during convalescence. No matter in what small quantities solid food may be given, it will create a gas which may be easily removed through the use of Champagne, giving comfort to the patient until such a time that the stomach will become strong enough to perform its functions without outside aid.

Since the year of 1870, the following crops have been shipped as vintages: 1870, 1874, 1878, 1880, 1884, 1889, 1892, 1893, 1898, 1899, 1900, 1904, 1906. All authentic vintage wines have the name and year of their production marked on cork and label.

NOILLY, PRAT & CO.'S
DRY
French Vermouth
MARSEILLES, FRANCE

IT
IMPARTS
JUST THE RIGHT
FLAVOR, CHARACTER
& QUALITY TO COCKTAILS
AND OTHER MIXED DRINKS
==

TAKEN WITH CARBON-
ATED WATER IT IS
A DELIGHTFUL
BEVERAGE

Clarets, Sauternes, Burgundies, Rhine and Moselle wines, are, next to champagne, more favorably known than any other, and while books could be written on their cultivation and maturing, I shall confine my remarks to their good uses and properties.

Red Burgundies are the richest of all natural wines, containing a great deal tannin or iron, and are for this reason a very fine blood building tonic.

Burgundies, being of very rich body, will form a sediment in the bottle, and before serving the same, should be carefully decanted, without the sediment becoming mixed with the wine, as this would render it bitter and unwholesome. Red Burgundies should be served with the dark meats, and at a temperature of about 65 degrees.

White Burgundies are served best at a temperature of about 50 degrees, and like Rhine, Moselle and Sauterne wines, should be used with the fish, oyster or white meat courses of the meal.

Clarets, although not as generally used as champagne, are nevertheless wines of excellent therapeutic value. Their low percentage of alcohol, combind with the tannin, forms a very good tonic in cases of consumption, anaemia, debility from overwork and indigestion. They are a beneficial and curative element. A glass served with your meals, properly assimilated with your food, has a stimulating and health giving effect.

Being the only wine not spoiled by the addition of water, a half a glass so diluted is the most refreshing type of a beverage, and a pleasure to your palate.

When serving claret with your meals, the lighter, but sound types should be served with the entree,

THE QUEEN OF TABLE WATERS

Apollinaris

Bottled only at the

Spring Neuenahr, Germany

And only with its on Natural Gas

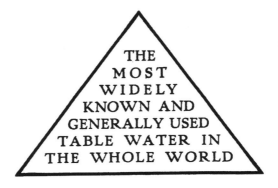

THE
MOST
WIDELY
KNOWN AND
GENERALLY USED
TABLE WATER IN
THE WHOLE WORLD

UNSURPASSED AS A MIXING WATER
AND FOR TABLE USES

while the rich and heavy chateau bottlings are served best with the roast.

They should be served at the temperature of the room in which the meal is served and like the Red Burgundies, they form sediment and should be carefully decanted.

A good many of the finer class are bottled at the vineyard in which they are grown, and are thus known as chateau bottlings.

Authentic chateau bottlings have their vintage and crest of the chateau plainly marked on cork and label.

The best vintages in the last forty years are as follows: 1870, 1874, 1875, 1877, 1878, 1888, 1893, 1899, 1904.

Sauternes, no doubt on account of their sweetness, are not being given their deserved appreciation. Yet, a better and finer wine, than a chateau Yquem of a good vintage could not be found the world over.

Sauternes are of a delicate flavor, pale golden color, mellow, rich and have fine, agreeable bouquet.

They are hygienic, not heady, and merit the description of perfection in white wines. Their relatively high alcoholic strength is both tonic and stimulating.

Consumed moderately, they are invaluable to convalescents after a severe illness, or when it is necessary to revive an organism extenuated by high fever, hemorrhage, or long fatigue.

For table service, the dry Sauternes should be served with the fish course while the rich and heavy Yquems are perfect dessert wines, and one or two glasses at the end of the meal facilitate digestion and provoke gaiety.

When conditioning Sauternes for the table, they

should be chilled slowly, and be served at a temperature of not below 42 degrees.

A good many Sauternes are bottled at the chateau, and to be authentic, should be properly marked on cork and label.

The best vintages in recent years are: 1864, 1865, 1869, 1874, 1884, 1887, 1893, 1899, 1904.

Rhine and Moselle wines have in late years greatly gained in favor, and when the qaulities and fineness of these wines are to be taken into consideration, their increased popularity is well deserved.

Rhine wines have great fragrance and vinosity and are pre-eminently the wines most suitable for intellectual enjoyment, as they are particularly exhilarating and increase the appetite. '

Being of light alcoholic strength, but rich in volatile ethers, they are exceedingly efficacious, and do not (like clarets) so quickly spoil after opening.

The finer qualities widely differ in flavor, and being rich in ethers are much valued as a stimulant in sustaining the nervous force of the heart while its enfeebled muscular tissue recuperates.

For serious nervous prostration their value as a remedy can hardly be overestimated, their beneficial effects being strikingly exhibited in bringing back a stronger and steadier heart beat, thus calming any attendant irritability which is of the utmost importance to the patient.

Moselle wines are of a quite distinct character, fine, of a grape flavor, very light and delicate, decidedly fruity and known to be a most wholesome and refreshing beverage.

The finest growth of the Moselle and its tributary, the River Saar, are Scharzhofberger, Scharzberger, Berncasteler Doctor, Brauneberger, Josephs-

ANGOSTURA BITTERS

Goes twice as far as any
other kind and adds better
quality to the beverage

THE GENUINE

Product of
J. G. B. SIEGERT & SONS

___

FLAVOR
QUALITY
STRENGTH
ECONOMY

___

*Used by the leading clubs,
hotels, cafes, bars, buffets,
the world over.*

hofer, etc., all widely known for their most delicate bouquet.

Moselle as a highly etheral wine is also very useful in cases of cerebral and cardiac exhaustion; it stimulates the action of the liver and kidneys, and is generally credited with being otherwise beneficial. It is anti-diabetic and does not increase the gouty tendency.

In conditioning either Rhine or Moselle wines for the table, they should be chilled slowly to a temperature of from 45 to 50 degrees.

In this way they retain all their quality.

The proper time to serve them is with the fish course of your dinner.

A good general rule to adopt in the serving of the different pure grape wines is:

Dark meat ....dark wine
White meat ....white wine

The best vintage in recent years in the Rhine and Moselle districts are as follows: 1886, 1893, 1895, 1897, 1900, 1904, 1906.

WHEN TO SERVE BEVERAGES.

Appetizers—Pale dry Sherry with Bitters, Vermouth, Dubonnet or Cocktail.

With Soup—Old Dry Sherry.

With Fish—Rhine Wine, Moselle, Sauternes, White Burgundy.

Entree—Light Bordeaux Claret.

Roast—Chateau bottled Claret or Red Burgundy.

Game—Vintage Champagne.

Pastry—Rich Madeira.

Cheese—Port.

Fruit—Tokay, Malaga, White Port.

Coffee—Cognac, Liqueurs or Cordials.

PORT.

The wine commonly known as "Port," is grown along the River Douro, in Portugal, where the same is known as "Vinho do Porto."

On the banks of this river, not far from the city of Oporto, are the vineyards of the Alto Douro.

The vineyards are built in terraces, resembling mammoth stairways, on the steps of which are planted the vines. A great variety of grapes are grown here, and the vintage begins about the middle of September.

Only perfectly ripe grapes are gathered by the army of women performing this work. The pressing of the grapes is very similar to the method used in the Sherry district of Spain.

The fermentation of the must begins almost immediately after the same has been transferred into the casks, but in the production of the richer wines, fermentation is stopped at an early stage, by the addition of young French brandy.

The wines intended for dry Ports are allowed to ferment more thoroughly before brandy is added.

When the secondary fermentation is complete, the casks are transported to the cellars of the shipping firms, most of whom are located at Oporto.

Wines from the perfect crops are sold as vintage wines, and a great many are shipped to England, where, at the age of from three to five years, they are bottled.

Port greatly improves in bottles, and care should be taken to use only the very best corks.

Bottles should be hermetically sealed either with wax or especially made caps. A well aged bottle of Port should be carefully decanted before serving, as

"The Whiskey Without a Headache"

is sold in more places and called for by name by more people, at the bars, in public and private clubs and best hotels than any other brand in the world.

Used for fifteen years by the United States Public Health & Marine Hospital Service.

Triumphant in every entry at Nine International Expositions and Fairs.   *All This Spells Quality*

COPYRIGHT 1899 OWNED BY J. W. MC CULLOCH, OWENSBORO, KY

GREEN RIVER DISTILLING CO., Owensboro, Ky.

a good deal of the tannin and tartar settles during maturation.

Port wine, of good quality and old, taken in moderation, is the most wholesome wine produced.

Port is especially agreeable when taken with a light repast, biscuit or cake. For those in delicate health, a glass of Port taken with a repast is a splendid invigorator, and will be found very beneficial to those suffering from anaemia.

SHERRY.

The district of Jerez, from which the well-known Spanish wines derive their name of "Sherry," is situated southwest from Jerez de la Frontera to Port St. Mary and north to San Lucar. The principal grapes grown in the Sherry producing districts are the Pedro Jimenez, Palomino, Penimo, Marituo Castellano.

The vintage begins in early September. The grapes are gathered into wooden troughs, and crushed by the bare feet of the workmen, after which they are pressed in an old-fashioned wooden press, from which the juice is pumped into large casks.

Previous to this operation, however, a small quantity of sulphate of lime is sprinkled upon the crushed grapes. This sulphate of lime is produced by burning some native earth, found near Jerez.

It is this process which gives the wine its peculiar flavor and develops its volatile ethers, the aroma.

The first racking of the wine takes place in June.

The wines are now stored in large casks in the bodegas, where in the course of one or two years remarkable changes are brought about, some of the wines developing into Amontillado, others into Olo-

THE WINE THAT'S ALL CHAMPAGNE

Paul Garrett

SPECIAL—DRY

Champagne

Every glassful sparkles with the life from the best of grapes grown in America's choicest vineyards.

DELICATE FLAVOR
FRAGRANT BOUQUET
PLEASING DRYNESS

Matured and naturally fermented in the bottle

———

GARRETT & CO.
NORFOLK, VA.

roso, Basto or Fino, although being made from the same grapes and all receiving the same treatment.

Amontillados are extremely dry, and of wonderful flavor.

Oloroso has a pronounced nutty flavor, darker in color, and heavier body.

Basto is the cheapest grade, and not generally shipped.

In very good years a few casks of wine are kept for the purpose of blending with wines produced in inferior seasons, this imparting to them flavor and body.

Wines kept in storage for this purpose are known as "Soleras," which themselves are replenished by wines from perfect vintages only.

Sherries, possessing a large amount of alcohol, greatly improve with age, and a properly matured old Sherry is unquestionably the peer of any wine. Genuine Sherry, on account of its freedom from acidity and sugar, has great dietetic value.

By those who suffer from indigestion, exhaustion, sleeplessness, and general debility, Sherry, properly used, will be found a wonderful tonic.

MADEIRA.

The island of Madeira is the largest of a group belonging to Portugal about five hundred miles southwest of Lisbon and is known for its excellent quality of wine.

The grapes mostly cultivated in the production of Madeira are the Malvasia, Vidogua, Sercial, Muscatel, Alicante, Negiamal, and Batardo.

The process of making Madeira wine is the same as applied in the making of Sherries.

ESTABLISHED   IN 1797

Schweppes

Soda Water, Ginger Ale, Sarsaparilla, Etc.

Made and Bottled in Great Britain

FURNISHED TO

H. M. KING GEO. V
H. M. the late King Edward VII
H. M. the late Queen Victoria
H. M. KING OF SPAIN

Used in the most exclusive Clubs, Hotels, Restaurants and Bars throughout the world

The gathered grapes are put into troughs and crushed by the naked feet of the harvesters.

The juice, or mosto, is transferred into large casks and allowed to ferment, after which the alcoholic percentage is increased, through the addition of French brandy.

This is done to better preserve the quality of the wine.

After the first racking, more brandy is added, this bringing the alcoholic percentage of the wine up to about 18 to 20 per cent.

The casks are then removed to the estufas, or heated storage, where they are left for several months.

The heating process assists the formation of ethers, and also destroys all chances for the growth of fungi, which would render the wine bitter and unpalatable.

Another way to properly mature the finer wines, and which is still in practice by a good many growers, is to send wines in casks on long sea voyages, where the intense heat and constant shaking has a very beneficial effect.

The storing of the casks of wine in the sun also has a beneficial effect, in the proper assimilation and formation of the ethers.

The best grades of Madeira wines are the Malmsey, Bual and Sercial.

Madeiras possess invigorating properties, and as either an appetizer or tonic are unsurpassed.

INDEX TO RECIPES

All mixed drinks are set in alphabetical order.

Classic Cocktail Resource Guide

Some ingredients found in vintage cocktail guides are unavailable or hard to come by today. However, the creation of historically accurate cocktails is a growing hobby, and with a bit of Internet research, you will find recipes for bitters and syrups online, as well as manufacturers that are developing new product lines for the classic cocktail enthusiast.

Vendors

A short selection of online vendors selling bitters, mixers, syrups, wine, liqueurs, and spirits. This list is by no means complete but is a good place to start your search.

BevMo!
www.bevmo.com

Binny's Beverage Depot
www.binnys.com

The Bitter Truth
www.the-bitter-truth.com

Cocktail Kingdom
www.cocktailkingdom.com

Fee Brothers
www.feebrothers.com

Hi-Time Wine Cellars
www.hitimewine.net

Internet Wines and Spirits
www.internetwines.com

The Jug Shop
www.thejugshop.com

Monin Gourmet Flavorings
www.moninstore.com

The Whiskey Exchange
www.thewhiskyexchange.com

General Interest

These sites provide background information on individual ingredients, suggestions for substitutes, current commercial availability, and recipes.

The Chanticleer Society
A Worldwide Organization of Cocktail Enthusiasts
www.chanticleersociety.org

Drink Boy
Adventures in Cocktails
www.drinkboy.com

The Internet Cocktail Database Ingredients Search
www.cocktaildb.com/ingr_search

Museum of the American Cocktail
www.museumoftheamericancocktail.org

WebTender Wiki
www.wiki.webtender.com

Coming Soon from
Classic Cocktail Guides
and Retro Bartender Books

Cocktails: How to Make Them

An 1898 Bartender's Guide

Livermore & Knight

ISBN: 978-1-880954-35-5

Classic Cocktail Guides
and Retro Bartender Books

Oxford Night Caps

A Collection of Recipes for Making Various Cups, Beverages, and Cocktails Used in the University

Richard Cook

ISBN: 978-1-880954-38-6

Classic Cocktail Guides
and Retro Bartender Books

Jack's Manual of Recipes for Fancy Mixed Drinks and How to Serve Them

A Pre-Prohibition Cocktail Book

J. A. Grohusko

ISBN: 978-1-880954-28-7

Classic Cocktail Guides
and Retro Bartender Books

Stuart's Fancy Drinks and How to Mix Them

Containing Clear and Practical Directions for
Mixing All Kinds of Cocktails, Sours, Egg Nog,
Sherry Cobblers, Coolers, Absinthe, Crustas,
Fizzes, Flips, Juleps, Fixes, Punches, Lemonades,
Pousse Cafes, Invalids' Drinks, Etc. Etc.

Thomas Stuart

ISBN: 978-1-880954-34-8

What to Drink

Non-Alcoholic Drinks and Cocktails
Served During Prohibition

Bertha E. L. Stockbridge

ISBN: 978-1-880954-36-2

Classic Cocktail Guides
and Retro Bartender Books

Nineteenth-Century Cocktail Creations

How to Mix Drinks: A Bar Keeper's Handbook

George Winter

ISBN: 978-1-880954-30-0